ESCOFFIER KITCHEN HANDBOOKS

HORS D'OEUVRE

ESCOFFIER KITCHEN HANDBOOKS

HORS D'OEUVRE

Selected and Edited by
Anne Johnson

CONSULTANT EDITORS
H.L.CRACKNELL & R.J.KAUFMANN

THE KINGSWOOD PRESS

The Kingswood Press
an imprint of William Heinemann Limited
10 Upper Grosvenor Street
London W1X 9PA

LONDON   MELBOURNE
JOHANNESBURG   AUCKLAND

Adapted from:
The Complete Guide to the Art of Modern Cookery
by A.Escoffier
translated by H.L.Cracknell and R.J.Kaufmann
(London: Heinemann, 1979)

Printed in Spain

ISBN 0 434 23903 8

Acknowledgements
Editors Andrew Jefford, Norma MacMillan
Art Editor Alyson Kyles
Production Shane Lask

Illustrations by Christine Robins/The Garden Studio

NOTES

1. Metric and imperial measurements have been calculated
separately, and are approximate rather than exact equivalents.
Therefore use only one set of measurements, either metric or
imperial, when preparing the recipes.

2. Words printed in *italics* in the recipes indicate that the word is
included in the short Glossary on page 109.

CONTENTS

INTRODUCTION

*T*he name 'hors d'oeuvre' – meaning, literally, outside the work – clearly defined their place in the classic menu. They formed an adjunct to a meal and, if omitted from such a menu, did not substantially alter its harmony and balance. In Escoffier's day, cold hors d'oeuvre were used to begin lunch menus, while hot hors d'oeuvre were customarily served after the soup course and before the run of main courses in dinner menus. As such, the hors d'oeuvre did not constitute a complete, independent course, and were seen (especially in the dinner menu) as optional. Nowadays, of course, the term hors d'oeuvre refers more widely to the starter or first course of a three- or more course meal.

Hors d'oeuvre are composed of ingredients of a light and delicate nature. They should not be served in enormous quantities, which might impair the appetite for the rest of the meal. What they lack in quantity, they should make up for in quality of flavour and presentation.

The recipes for hors d'oeuvre in this book have been divided, following Escoffier's example, into cold and hot dishes, and the book ends with a chapter of basic recipes used in the preparation of many of the hors d'oeuvre.

COLD
HORS D'OEUVRE

Hors d'Oeuvre Froids

C old hors d'oeuvre, today as in Escoffier's day, are particularly well suited to lunch-time eating and entertaining. Preparation can generally be done in advance; many of the dishes have a pleasing, colourful appearance; and the highly defined flavours of cold hors d'oeuvre work best in the context of a lunchtime meal.

There is no limit to the number of possible hors d'oeuvre, and those that follow will suggest many more to the imaginative cook. Escoffier himself drew attention to the skills required to create good hors d'oeuvre: a sure sense of taste, a creative bent and an artistic touch. Diligent practice in this area will soon pay dividends: these are qualities central to all cookery expertise.

Allumettes aux Anchois

100 g (4 oz) Feuilletage, page 98
anchovy essence
75 g (3 oz) canned anchovy fillets, drained

Farce de Poisson
100 g (4 oz) fish, such as salmon, trout, whiting or sole,
free from skin and bone
salt
white pepper
$\frac{1}{2}$ egg white
120 ml (4 fl oz) double cream

*F*irst, make the Farce de Poisson. Pound the fish with the seasonings, then add the half egg white. Beat well with a spatula, then pass through a fine sieve. Alternatively, process in a food processor.

Place the fish purée in a shallow pan or basin, smooth it over with a spatula and refrigerate for at least 2 hours. Then mix in the cream gradually and carefully until it has been completely incorporated.

Roll out a band of pastry dough approximately 7.5 cm (3 inches) wide by 3 mm ($\frac{1}{8}$ inch) thick. Spread with a thin layer of Farce de Poisson seasoned with anchovy essence.

Cut into rectangles 2.5 cm (1 inch) wide and place on a baking sheet. Arrange fillets of anchovy on top of the forcemeat, either lengthways or trellis fashion.

Bake in a hot oven (220°C, 425°F, Gas Mark 7) for about 12 minutes.

MAKES 20

Anchois Frais Marinés

450 g (1 lb) fresh anchovies
coarse sea salt
oil for deep frying
1 shallot, peeled and finely chopped
3 parsley stalks, 1 pinch thyme and 1 bay leaf
salt and pepper
juice of 2 lemons
6 tablespoons olive oil

Clean the anchovies well, pack in salt and leave for 2 hours. Clean the salt from the anchovies, then plunge them into very hot oil (190°C, 375°F) for a few minutes, to stiffen them. Drain. Mix together the remaining ingredients and add the anchovies. Leave to marinate in the refrigerator for 2–3 days. Serve in a dish with a little of the marinade.

SERVES 6

Anchois aux Poivrons

16 salted anchovy fillets
olive oil
2 medium-sized green or sweet red peppers
3 hard-boiled eggs, shelled and chopped
2 tablespoons chopped fresh parsley
50 g (2 oz) capers

Clean the salt off the anchovy fillets, then wash and dry them. Marinate in olive oil for 2–3 hours. Meanwhile, grill the peppers until charred, peel off their skins and cut into strips. Drain the anchovy fillets and arrange in a *ravier*, alternating with strips of pepper. Garnish with the remaining ingredients.

SERVES 6–8

Anchois des Tamarins

16 salted anchovy fillets
100 g (4 oz) fillet of white fish, such as cod, haddock or halibut,
poached or steamed
150 ml ($\frac{1}{4}$ pint) Sauce Mayonnaise, page 107
1 teaspoon cayenne pepper
450 g (1 lb) potatoes, peeled
3 tablespoons oil
1 tablespoon wine vinegar
1 tablespoon chopped fresh fines herbes
16 black olives

Clean the salt off the anchovy fillets, then wash, dry and lightly flatten them. Mash the cooked fish, then make into a purée with the Sauce Mayonnaise, and season with cayenne pepper. Spread the fish purée thinly over the anchovy fillets and roll up into *paupiettes*.

Cook the potatoes in lightly salted boiling water, keeping them slightly firm. Grate these, while still warm, down the centre of a dish. Season with the oil and vinegar, and sprinkle with the chopped *fines herbes*. Arrange the paupiettes on each side of the potato and put an olive on top of each one.

SERVES 6–8

Anguille au Vin Blanc et Paprika

750 g–1 kg (1½–2 lb) eels
salt
2 onions, peeled and sliced into rings
1 bouquet garni
4 cloves garlic, peeled
4 peppercorns
1 teaspoon paprika
600 ml (1 pint) white wine
50 ml (2 fl oz) brandy
40 g (1½ oz) butter
25 g (1 oz) flour

Clean the eels and wash in salted water. Cut into sections about 7.5 cm (3 inches) long. Arrange in a shallow pan with the sliced onions, bouquet garni, garlic, a pinch of salt, the peppercorns and paprika. Moisten with the white wine and bring to the boil. Add the brandy, flame, cover and continue cooking for about 45 minutes or until tender.

When the eel is cooked, allow it to cool in the cooking liquor. Remove the pieces of eel, discard the skin and detach the fillets from the central bone; place these eel fillets neatly in a suitable dish.

Skim off any fat from the cooking liquor and thicken with a *beurre manié*, made from the butter and flour. Pass this sauce through a fine strainer over the eel, then place in a cool place and allow to set.

SERVES 6–8

Artichauts à la Grecque

24 very small young artichokes
salt

Marinade
1 litre (1¾ pints) water
150 ml (¼ pint) oil
juice of 3 lemons
salt
50 g (2 oz) fennel, trimmed and cut into small bâtons
50 g (2 oz) celery, trimmed and cut into small bâtons
10 coriander seeds
10 peppercorns
1 sprig thyme
2 bay leaves

C hoose very small artichokes, making sure they have not developed chokes. Trim and cut off the tips of the leaves, then blanch in boiling salted water and refresh under cold running water.

Place all the marinade ingredients in a pan and bring to the boil for a few minutes. Add the artichokes and simmer gently for 15 minutes.

Allow the artichokes to cool in the marinade, and serve very cold with a little of the marinade.

Other vegetables that may be prepared in exactly the same way include small celery sticks, cut into 2 or 4 according to size; bulbs of fennel, quartered or halved according to size; and leeks, cut into 7.5 cm (3 inch) lengths.

SERVES 8

Fonds d'Artichauts Garnis

12 small artichokes
salt
1 tablespoon chopped fresh parsley, to garnish

Marinade
150 ml ($\frac{1}{4}$ pint) oil
500 ml (18 fl oz) wine vinegar
1 pinch thyme
6 peppercorns
4 parsley stalks

Filling
225 g (8 oz) soft herring roes
50 g (2 oz) butter

B reak off the artichoke stems close to the leaves and discard any dry or discoloured leaves. Trim the tips of the leaves and cook the artichokes in boiling salted water for 20–30 minutes, or until a leaf comes away easily.

Drain upside-down. Pull off the leaves and discard. Remove the choke and discard. Marinate the artichoke hearts in oil and vinegar, seasoned with thyme, pepper and parsley, for 1–2 hours. Meanwhile, stew the herring roes gently in the butter, then pass through a fine sieve.

Remove the artichoke hearts from the marinade and top each one with a little puréed herring roe. Garnish with chopped parsley.

SERVES 4–6

Betterave en Salade

1.5 kg (3 lb) beetroots
450 g (1 lb) onions
1 tablespoon chopped fresh parsley and chervil

Dressing
6 tablespoons oil
2 tablespoons wine vinegar
salt
pepper

Bake the beetroots and onions in a moderately hot oven (190°C, 375°F, Gas Mark 5) for about 45 minutes or until cooked but still fairly firm.

Allow both the beetroots and onions to cool, then peel and slice each finely into *julienne*. Mix the beetroot and onion with the oil and vinegar, then season with salt and pepper. Arrange in a *ravier* and sprinkle with the chopped parsley and chervil.

An alternative salad, **Betterave en Salade à la Crème**, can be made by preparing the onion and beetroot as above, then dressing with Sauce Moutarde à la Crème, page 107.

SERVES 8

Canapés

Canapés or toasts are made from bread cut into various shapes and sizes, and no more than 5 mm ($\frac{1}{4}$ inch) thick. These are then either fried in clarified butter or, more usually, toasted.

The garnish for a canapé usually consists of only one main ingredient, such as marinated fish, anchovy, fillets of herring, and so on. A combination of ingredients is, however, quite acceptable, provided that the flavours are in harmony.

The best sort of garnish for canapés consists of fresh butter mixed with a purée of – or very finely chopped – meat, poultry, shellfish, fish or cheese. Butter-based toppings are best placed on top of the toast with a piping bag and a fancy tube. Whatever the garnish, the toast should always be buttered while it is still hot so as to keep it soft.

Canapés au Caviar

4 slices white bread
75 g (3 oz) butter, softened
50 g (2 oz) caviare
1 onion, peeled and very finely chopped

Beurre de Caviar
15 g ($\frac{1}{2}$ oz) caviare
50 g (2 oz) butter, softened

*F*irst prepare the caviare butter. Finely pound the caviare in a basin until smooth, then add the softened butter and mix well. Toast the bread and cut into 5 cm (2 inch) diameter rounds with a plain pastry cutter. Spread with caviare butter while hot. Pipe a border of softened butter around the edges, using a small fancy tube. Place caviare in the centres, and serve a dish of finely chopped onion separately.

MAKES 16

Canapés à la Danoise

50 g (2 oz) herring fillet
100 ml (3½ fl oz) dry white wine
12 slices brown bread
50 g (2 oz) smoked salmon, finely sliced
50 g (2 oz) caviare

Beurre de Raifort
25 g (1 oz) horseradish, peeled and grated
120 g (4½ oz) butter, softened

Marinate the herring fillet for a few hours in the white wine, then drain and slice finely. Meanwhile, prepare the horseradish butter by mixing the grated horseradish with the softened butter and passing through a fine sieve, or working to a soft paste in a food processor.

Heat the slices of brown bread in a cool oven (150°C, 300°F, Gas Mark 2) until warm but still soft. Coat them with the prepared horseradish butter while still warm and cover this with alternate strips of smoked salmon, herring fillet and lines of caviare. Finally, carefully cut out the garnished slices with a plain oval cutter.

MAKES 24–36

Canapés à l'Ecarlate

20 slices white bread
100 g (4 oz) cooked salt ox tongue, thinly sliced

Beurre de Moutarde
1 tablespoon Dijon mustard
150 g (5 oz) butter, softened

*P*repare the mustard butter by mixing the mustard with the butter. Toast the slices of bread and allow to cool, then spread with a layer of mustard-flavoured butter half the thickness of the bread. Cover this with very thin slices of cooked salt ox tongue.

Allow the butter to set firm in a cool place, then cut the canapés into shapes with a star-shaped cutter dipped into boiling water. Pipe a little decoration of mustard butter in the centre of each one.

MAKES 40–60

Céleri à la Bonne Femme

3–4 sticks celery, weighing about 225 g (8 oz) in all
225 g (8 oz) dessert apples, peeled, cored and quartered
300 ml ($\frac{1}{2}$ pint) Sauce Moutarde à la Crème, page 107

*S*lice the celery finely across the stalks, then finely slice the apples. Mix together with the Sauce Moutarde à la Crème and serve promptly.

SERVES 4–6

Salade de Céleri-rave

500 g (1¼ lb) celeriac, peeled
10 g (⅓ oz) dry mustard
a few drops lemon juice
150 ml (¼ pint) double cream
1 pinch salt
freshly ground black pepper

Cut the raw celeriac into thick *julienne*. Mix the mustard and lemon juice in a basin then add the cream, blending thoroughly together. Season with salt and flavour well with freshly ground black pepper. Mix the celeriac well with the sauce.

Instead of serving the celeriac with the mustard and cream sauce described above, it may also be served with a Sauce Vinaigrette, lightly flavoured with mustard.

A **Salade de Céleri** can be made by cutting stalks of tender young celery into short lengths, then scoring each length finely with a sharp knife without cutting right through. Place the scored lengths of celery in iced water to curl up, then drain well and serve with the dressing above.

SERVES 4—6

Cèpes Marinés

1 kg (2¼ lb) small ceps

Marinade
500 ml (18 fl oz) wine vinegar
150 ml (¼ pint) oil
1 clove garlic, peeled and crushed
1 pinch thyme
1 bay leaf, crushed
6 peppercorns
1 pinch ground coriander
1 pinch fennel seeds
4 stalks parsley

*B*lanch the mushrooms for 7–8 minutes in boiling water, then drain and allow to cool. Meanwhile, prepare the marinade. Combine all the ingredients in a pan, bring to the boil and simmer very gently for 10 minutes.

Place the mushrooms in an earthenware or similar terrine and strain the boiling marinade over them. Allow to cool, then place to marinate in the refrigerator for 8 days. Serve the mushrooms with a little of the marinade spooned over them.

SERVES 8

Cerises au Vinaigre

1 kg (2¼ lb) unripe Morello cherries
3 cloves
1 small piece cinnamon
1 pinch grated nutmeg
1 pinch tarragon
1 litre (1¾ pints) wine vinegar
200 g (7 oz) brown sugar

Remove the stalks from the cherries. Place the cherries in preserving jars containing the cloves, cinnamon, nutmeg and tarragon. Boil the vinegar with the sugar, allow to cool and pour over the cherries.

Leave for 15 days, then serve with a little of the marinade.

SERVES 8–10

Cervelles Robert

4 pairs lambs' brains
Court-bouillon au Vinaigre, page 108
300 ml (½ pint) Sauce Moutarde à la Crème, page 107
1 small stick celery, trimmed and finely sliced in julienne

Place the brains under gently running cold water to remove as much of the blood as possible. Remove all the skin and membranes and re-soak to remove the remaining blood, then poach the brains for 15 minutes in a vinegar court-bouillon. Drain and allow to cool, then cut into small slices. Trim them neatly and arrange in raviers.

Purée the brain trimmings and add to the Sauce Moutarde à la Crème along with the fine julienne of celery.

SERVES 6

Choux Rouges

1 medium red cabbage, weighing about 1 kg (2¼ lb)
wine vinegar to cover
225 g (8 oz) dessert apples, peeled, cored and sliced
salt
pepper

*F*inely shred the cabbage and marinate in vinegar for about 6 hours. Drain and add the sliced apples. Season with salt and pepper, and toss well.

SERVES 8–10

Paupiettes de Choux Verts

1 green cabbage, weighing about 1 kg (2¼ lb)
salt
225 g (8 oz) cooked long-grain rice, seasoned and lightly dressed
in single cream and lemon juice
pepper
olive oil

*C*ook the large green cabbage leaves in boiling salted water, keeping them slightly firm. Refresh under cold running water, drain well and cut into rectangles.

Cover each rectangle with a thin layer of the seasoned and dressed rice. Season with salt and pepper and roll into *paupiettes*.

Arrange the paupiettes in *raviers* and sprinkle with a little olive oil just before serving.

SERVES 8

Concombres à la Danoise

2 large cucumbers
225 g (8 oz) smoked salmon
225 g (8 oz) smoked herring
3 hard-boiled eggs, shelled

To garnish
a little grated horseradish

Cut the cucumbers into halves, and then into sections; scoop out the seeds from the middle of each section, then trim each section into rounded, boat-shaped barquettes. Purée the smoked salmon, dice the herring and finely chop the hard-boiled eggs; mix together carefully. Then fill the centres of the cucumber cases with this mixture and sprinkle the surface of the stuffed cucumbers with a little grated horseradish.

SERVES 6

Concombres Farcis

2 large cucumbers
6 tablespoons olive oil
2 tablespoons wine vinegar
250 g (9 oz) diced Macédoine, page 32, or a rice salad,
pages 41–46

Cut the cucumbers into halves, and then into sections. Scoop out the seeds from the middle of each section, then trim each section into rounded, boat-shaped barquettes.

Blanch, refresh, drain and then marinate the barquettes for 45 minutes in the oil and vinegar. Remove, then fill their centres with Macédoine or rice salad.

SERVES 6

Concombres en Salade

1 or 2 cucumbers, depending on size
fine salt

Dressing
2 tablespoons wine vinegar
6 tablespoons olive oil
pepper

To garnish
2 tablespoons chopped fresh chervil

P eel the cucumbers, cut them in half lengthwise and remove their seeds. Finely slice the cucumber halves, sprinkle with fine salt and leave for 25–30 minutes so as to extract some of the moisture from the slices.

Drain well and arrange in a *ravier*. To prepare the dressing, place the vinegar in a mixing bowl and gradually incorporate the oil, whisking all the time or beating with a fork. Season with pepper. Do not add salt as the slices of cucumber will already be quite salty. Pour the dressing over the prepared cucumber just before serving. Sprinkle generously with the chopped chervil and serve.

SERVES 6

Crèmes pour Hors d'Oeuvre

By mixing pounded smoked salmon, caviare, tuna fish or game with double cream, it is possible to make some very fine creams which may be used as fillings, stuffings and spreads in the preparation of hors d'oeuvre. Below is a recipe for a smoked salmon cream, but remember that there are other possibilities for different flavourings as indicated above.

It is also possible to make a variety of small and delicate hors d'oeuvre by mixing the chosen cream with a few tablespoons of melted aspic jelly in keeping with the basic ingredient before adding the cream. This mixture is then placed in small, lightly oiled, fancy moulds – the moulds used for making petits fours are highly suitable for this purpose. Allow to set in a cool place and demould at the last moment on to a suitable dish.

Crème au Saumon Fumé

225 g (8 oz) smoked salmon
2 tablespoons thick fresh cream
cayenne pepper
a few drops lemon juice
6 tablespoons double or whipping cream, stiffly whipped

Finely pound the smoked salmon or work it in a food processor until smooth. Stir in the thick cream, adding a little at a time. Season with cayenne pepper and lemon juice and fold in the whipped cream to finish. Use to fill cold barquettes or bouchées, or hollowed, poached vegetables; or set and mould with fish aspic as described above.

MAKES 350 G (12 OZ) CREAM

Escabèche de Rouget

1.25 kg (2½ lb) red mullet, cleaned
flour
500 ml (18 fl oz) oil
8 cloves garlic
2 small carrots, peeled, grooved and thinly sliced
2 small onions, peeled and cut into thin rings
300 ml (½ pint) vinegar
150 ml (¼ pint) water
1 pinch coarse salt
1 sprig thyme
½ bay leaf
5 parsley stalks
2 small chilli peppers

E scabèche, which is of Spanish origin, is a spicy dish of fried fish, marinated and served cold. It can be made using a variety of different fish, according to availability, including smelts, sardines or, as here, red mullet.

Dry the fish, flour them lightly then colour on both sides in a little of the oil. Drain well and arrange in a deep dish. Set aside.

Add the rest of the oil to the pan and reheat until lightly smoking. Add the unpeeled cloves of garlic and the sliced onion and carrot. Fry for a few minutes, allowing the vegetables to colour very slightly, then set aside to cool.

When cool, add the vinegar, water, salt, herbs and chilli peppers to the pan. Bring to the boil, simmer very gently for 12 minutes, then pour over the fish while still hot. When cool, place in the refrigerator and allow to marinate for 24 hours.

Serve the fish very cold with a little of the marinade and the sliced vegetables.

SERVES 8

Fruits de Mer

Under this name come all types of salt-water shellfish which can be served, raw or cooked, as a selection on their own as an hors d'oeuvre. Oysters are usually an exception here: their quality as an hors d'oeuvre is such that they are served on their own when raw and garnished in a simple yet appropriate way. There is only one prerequisite for the serving of Fruits de Mer, which is that the shellfish be absolutely fresh.

The **Assiette** or **Plateau de Fruits de Mer**, or seafood platter, is a princely selection chosen from among clams, winkles, mussels, cockles, sea urchins, prawns, shrimps, langoustines, crab and lobster. (An exclusively raw selection will not include crustaceans.) It is served on a bed of crushed ice and garnished with lemon wedges and sprigs of parsley or seaweed. It should be accompanied by very thin slices of brown bread and butter.

The presentation is of the utmost importance. Shellfish lends itself particularly well to imaginative arrangements which do much to stimulate the tastebuds and consequently the appetite of guests. It should be remembered, though, that shellfish served on their own in this way make very light eating, whereas their shells are both weighty and bulky, so every effort should be made to ensure that each assiette contains a generous and wide-ranging selection.

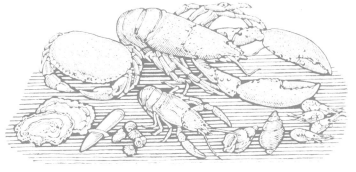

Harengs Lucas

12–16 small cooked smoked herrings, such as buckling
600 ml (1 pint) milk
6 hard-boiled egg yolks
1 tablespoon Dijon mustard
1 tablespoon wine vinegar
300 ml ($\frac{1}{2}$ pint) oil
1 tablespoon chopped shallot
2 tablespoons chopped fresh chervil
2 tablespoons chopped gherkin

Soak the smoked herrings in lukewarm water for about 1 hour, then drain, skin and fillet them. Place to soak in the milk for a further hour.

Meanwhile, prepare the sauce. Place the hard-boiled egg yolks in a basin and mix to a smooth paste. Add the mustard and vinegar and gradually stir in the oil, using a wooden spoon and adding it drop by drop, in much the same way as when making Sauce Mayonnaise, page 107. Finally, add the chopped shallot, chervil and gherkin, and season well.

Drain the milk from the herrings and pat dry. Arrange on a serving dish and pour the sauce over them.

SERVES 8

Harengs Roulés

12–16 small salted herrings
600 ml (1 pint) milk
2 tablespoons made English mustard
2 small onions, peeled and finely chopped
500 ml (18 fl oz) wine vinegar
1 bouquet garni
10 peppercorns
4 cloves
100 ml (3½ fl oz) oil

To garnish
1 large onion, peeled and thinly sliced into rings
2 tablespoons chopped fresh parsley
16 gherkins

Select firm, white-fleshed salted herrings with soft roes. Soak them in the milk for a few hours to remove the salt. Then drain and fillet the fish, removing as many bones as possible. Coat the inside surfaces of the fillets with the mustard mixed with half the chopped onion. Roll them up and tie with string. Arrange in an earthenware or similar dish with the roes.

Boil the vinegar with the bouquet garni, the remaining onion, the peppercorns and cloves. Strain the spicy vinegar over the fish while still boiling and allow to cool.

When cold, remove the fish. Pass the roes through a fine sieve or work in a food processor. Mix this purée back into the vinegar and add the oil.

Return the fish to this mixture and allow to marinate for 2–3 days. To serve, arrange the rollmops in *raviers* with a little of the marinade. Then garnish each ravier with the thinly sliced onion rings, the chopped parsley and several gherkins.

SERVES 8

Harengs à la Russe

750 g (1½ lb) potatoes, peeled
salt
12–16 smoked herrings, cooked and filleted

Dressing
6 tablespoons oil
2 tablespoons wine vinegar
pepper

To garnish
1 tablespoon chopped shallot
2 tablespoons chopped fresh chervil
2 tablespoons chopped fresh fennel
2 tablespoons chopped fresh tarragon

Cook the potatoes in lightly salted boiling water, keeping them on the firm side. When they are cooked drain well and when cold, slice them thinly.

Cut the fillets of smoked herring into thin slices. Arrange them in a dish, overlapping and alternating with slices of cooked potato.

Mix together the oil, vinegar and pepper, then pour this dressing over the fish and potatoes. Sprinkle with the chopped shallot and fresh herbs and serve.

Smoked herrings are sold prepared in various ways. Uncooked kippers are one of the most popular varieties of smoked herring, and can be bought either with the bone in or ready-boned. Buckling is a small smoked herring. It is smoked at a higher temperature than a kipper, so the flesh is lightly cooked during the smoking process. Bloaters are lightly smoked, dry salted, whole herrings. They do not keep for quite as long as other types of smoked herring and they should therefore be served within 24 hours of purchase.

SERVES 8

Huîtres

Always buy oysters from a reliable source so as to be as sure as possible that they are fresh. A tightly closed shell indicates freshness, and they can also be kept fresh in a refrigerator for a few hours, by placing them in a deep receptacle covered with wet cloth.

When the oysters are required, scrub and then open them: hold each oyster in a clean cloth in the palm of one hand, deeper shell down; prise open the shells at the hinge, working the point of the knife into the hinge, and cut the ligament. (Special knives are available for this purpose.) Remove the beard from each shell if preferred, then loosen the oysters, leaving them in the deeper half-shell with their juices. They must be served very cold, if possible on crushed ice.

Serve accompanied by thin slices of brown bread and butter with a **Sauce à la Mignonette** (vinegar well seasoned with fresh, coarsely ground pepper), and with lemon wedges.

Huîtres Natives au Caviar

12 small baked tartlet cases, made using Pâte à Foncer, page 96
75 g (3 oz) caviare
12 oysters, preferably from Whitstable or Colchester, opened and removed from shells
freshly ground pepper
½ lemon

*F*ill the tartlet cases with caviare, leaving a hollow in the centre. Place a bearded oyster, seasoned with pepper and a drop of lemon juice, in the hollow. Serve immediately.

SERVES 4–6

Macédoine

175 g (6 oz) pickling onions, peeled
175 g (6 oz) cauliflower florets, lightly blanched
175 g (6 oz) small fresh gherkins
175 g (6 oz) French beans, trimmed
175 g (6 oz) very small sweet red peppers
175 g (6 oz) artichoke hearts, blanched and sliced
300 ml ($\frac{1}{2}$ pint) wine vinegar
1 tablespoon Dijon mustard
salt

Place all the vegetables in a stoneware or glass jar. Bring the vinegar to the boil with the mustard and a little salt. Pour this over the vegetables and leave to marinate for 1–2 days so as to allow the flavours to mingle.

The term macédoine, meaning a mixture of vegetables, is derived from the name 'Macedonia', which was a South Balkan kingdom created in ancient times by Alexander the Great from various small states: the usage refers to the mixture of nationalities found there. The term can also refer to a fruit salad served in syrup or set in jelly.

SERVES 8

Maquereaux Marinés

6 small mackerel, cleaned
25 g (1 oz) butter
1 lemon, fluted and sliced

Marinade
600 ml (1 pint) dry white wine
300 ml ($\frac{1}{2}$ pint) wine vinegar
2 carrots, peeled, fluted and thinly sliced
4 small onions, peeled and sliced into rings
2 shallots, peeled and sliced
1 sprig thyme
2 bay leaves
4 parsley stalks
10 peppercorns
salt

First prepare the marinade. Mix all the ingredients together, bring to the boil and simmer gently for 10 minutes. Arrange the mackerel in a shallow buttered pan and cover with the boiling marinade. Poach them gently for 10–15 minutes and allow them to cool in the liquid. When they are cool, chill them further in the refrigerator.

Serve the mackerel very cold with a little marinade. Garnish with some of the carrot slices and onion rings, and with slices of fluted lemon.

This dish can also be prepared using fresh herrings. Mackerel are in season from October to July but are at their best during April, May and June. Herrings, on the other hand, are in season all year round but are best from June to December.

SERVES 6

Melon Frappé aux Vins Divers

1 large melon, preferably Cantaloup
250 ml (8 fl oz) Madeira, port, Marsala or brandy
2 tablespoons caster sugar

Make an incision around the stalk, about 9 cm (3½ inches) in diameter. Remove this piece and reserve for later. Scoop out the seeds and filaments, using a spoon, and pour in the Madeira, port, Marsala or brandy, according to taste. Add the caster sugar and replace the 'lid'. Place on crushed ice in the refrigerator to chill for 2–3 hours.

Present the melon whole at the table. Remove the lid and scoop out the flesh in shell-shaped pieces using a silver spoon. Arrange on iced plates with a little of the wine.

Instead of using a large whole melon as above, smaller sized melons such as the Charentais or Ogen varieties may be served as individual portions. Prepare them in exactly the same way as the large melon above, then present on crushed ice in individual glass dishes. The pieces of fruit may be eaten directly from the melon.

SERVES 4

Moelle de Végétaux Divers

*T*ender parts are found under the hard outer skins of some vegetable stems such as those of large artichokes, and the stumps of cabbage, cauliflower, broccoli and calabrese. It may come as a surprise to some people to learn of the potential of these hidden assets.

They can all be trimmed of their fibrous parts and used as a base for delicate salads; or they can be blanched in boiling salted water, refreshed under cold running water and prepared 'à la Grecque' in a court-bouillon. The stumps of curly endive and Batavian endive can also be prepared 'à la Grecque' in a court-bouillon after simply being washed and peeled. The following quantity of court-bouillon is suitable for at least 450 g (1 lb) trimmed vegetable stems.

Court-bouillon à la Grecque
1 litre (1¾ pints) water
150 ml (¼ pint) olive oil
juice of 3 lemons
salt
50 g (2 oz) fennel, trimmed and coarsely chopped
50 g (2 oz) celery, trimmed and coarsely sliced
10 coriander seeds
10 peppercorns
1 sprig thyme
2 bay leaves

*B*ring all the ingredients to the boil for a few minutes, add the chosen main ingredient and blanch quickly until just tender. Allow to cool in the liquid and serve very cold with a little of the court-bouillon.

SERVES 4

Salade de Moules et Céleri

1.75 litres (3 pints) mussels, cleaned
125 g (4½ oz) onion, peeled and sliced
15 g (½ oz) parsley stalks
pinch crushed peppercorns
200 ml (7 fl oz) water
1 small head crisp white celery, trimmed and very finely sliced
250 ml (8 fl oz) Sauce Moutarde à la Crème, page 107

Place the mussels in a deep pan with the onion, parsley stalks, crushed peppercorns and water, then cover and cook at high heat for 5–7 minutes until the shells have opened. Remove the mussels from the shells and remove the beards. Use only the mussels which have opened during cooking, discarding those that have remained closed.

Place the cooked mussels in a bowl with the finely sliced celery and toss lightly with the Sauce Moutarde à la Crème. The salad can either be served as it is in *raviers*, or the mussels can be replaced in half shells before arranging with the salad in individual serving dishes.

SERVES 6

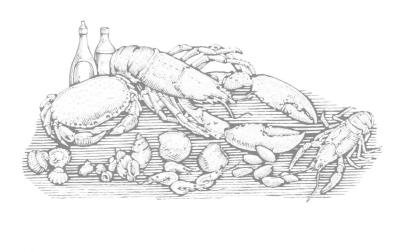

Oeufs Farcis

Hard-boiled eggs can be used in many ways for hors d'oeuvre, though they are best suited for stuffing with a wide range of purées, *salpicons* and salads. The most important aspect of their preparation is the inventiveness and artistry of the cook: a simple but well-thought-out idea is, in this respect, generally preferable to complex and elaborate presentation. Two suggestions for the preparation of stuffed eggs are given below.

Oeufs Farcis aux Champignons

Separate the whites and yolks of six hard-boiled eggs. Finely chop 100 g (4 oz) mushrooms and 1 small peeled shallot, then fry in 25 g (1 oz) butter until all the moisture has evaporated. Cool. Rub the egg yolks through a fine sieve, then mix with 25 g (1 oz) softened butter, 50 g (2 oz) curd cheese, and 85 ml (3 fl oz) Sauce Béchamel, page 102. Season carefully with salt and pepper. Mix in the mushroom and shallot mixture, then pipe into the egg whites. Top each stuffed egg with a tiny button mushroom, fried in butter and cooled.

SERVES 6

Oeufs Farcis aux Crevettes

Separate the whites and yolks of six hard-boiled eggs. Finely chop 100 g (4 oz) shelled cooked prawns. Rub the egg yolks through a fine sieve, then mix with 25 g (1 oz) softened butter, 50 g (2 oz) curd cheese, and 85 ml (3 fl oz) Sauce Béchamel, page 102. Season carefully with salt and cayenne pepper. Mix in the chopped prawns, then pipe into the egg whites. Top each stuffed egg with a shelled prawn.

SERVES 6

Pimentos à l'Algérienne

3—4 small red peppers
3 tablespoons olive oil
1 tablespoon wine vinegar
1 onion, peeled and finely sliced in rings

G rill the red peppers under a moderate heat until the skin blisters, then remove and discard the skin. Cut the peppers in half lengthways, discard the seeds and cut into *julienne*. Mix together the olive oil and wine vinegar, season, then pour over the peppers and toss well. Garnish with the onion.

SERVES 4

Poireaux Farcis

4 medium leeks
stuffing to taste (see below)

Marinade
6 tablespoons oil
2 tablespoons wine vinegar
salt
pepper

C ut the white of leek into 2.5—4 cm (1—1½ inch) lengths. Cook them lightly for 5—10 minutes in boiling water, keeping them fairly firm. Drain well. Combine the marinade ingredients, add the leeks, and marinate for 1—2 hours.

Remove the centre of the leeks to make small cylindrical cases and stuff with a filling of your choice, such as one of the rice salads, pages 41—46, mixed perhaps with a little extra chopped cooked meat or chicken.

SERVES 4

Radis

The common red radish is not used as an hors d'oeuvre as frequently as its quality merits. Radishes should be selected for firmness and plumpness, carefully trimmed at the top and tail and then placed whole to become crisp in iced water. (The cutting of radishes into fancy shapes is only suitable for garnishing purposes.) Serve radishes on crushed ice, accompanied with fine butter curls, salt and thin slices of brown bread or rye bread.

Radis Noirs

2–3 large black radishes, peeled and thinly sliced
salt

Dressing
3 tablespoons oil
1 tablespoon wine vinegar
pepper

Sprinkle the sliced radishes with salt and leave to marinate for 15–20 minutes. Drain well and dress with oil and vinegar, seasoned with pepper.

SERVES 4

Rougets au Safran

6 small red mullets, cleaned
olive oil
6 tomatoes
600 ml (1 pint) dry white wine
1 pinch salt
6 peppercorns
4 stalks parsley
1 tablespoon chopped fresh fennel
1 sprig thyme
1 bay leaf
1 clove garlic, crushed
10 coriander seeds
1 large pinch saffron threads

To garnish
1 lemon, fluted and sliced
sprigs of fennel

Put the fish in a well-oiled flameproof dish. Peel and core the tomatoes, remove the pips and chop the tomato flesh roughly. Place this around the mullets. Cover with white wine and add all the flavourings.

Bring to the boil, cover and place in a moderate oven (180°C, 350°F, Gas Mark 4). Monitor the oven temperature so as to ensure that the fish simmers very gently for 10–12 minutes, then remove from the oven and allow the fish to cool fully in the cooking liquid.

Serve with a little of the cooking liquid, vegetables and flavourings and garnish with slices of carefully fluted lemon and sprigs of fennel.

SERVES 6

Salades

The composition of salads for hors d'oeuvre is very flexible and depends to a large extent on the cook's personal preference and imagination. They can be arranged in *raviers* and garnished with a border of sliced cucumber, hard-boiled egg white or beetroot; they can be piled into emptied halves of tomato; or they can simply be placed on top of large slices of tomato or cucumber.

The number of ingredients that can be used is considerable. The following salads are all based on rice. This can be cooked in any way, the essential thing being that the cooked grains of rice should be well separated, which necessitates the use of a suitable long-grain type of rice such as Patna.

In this kind of salad, the rice constitutes about half the total amount, the other half being made up of all the other ingredients, proportionate to their suitability.

Salade Bergerette

350 g (12 oz) cooked long-grain rice
6 hard-boiled eggs, shelled and sliced
3 tablespoons chopped fresh chives
150 ml ($\frac{1}{4}$ pint) double cream, lightly whipped
salt
pepper
1 tablespoon grated horseradish, curry powder or made mustard
(optional)

Combine the cooked rice, sliced hard-boiled eggs, chives and whipped cream. Season with salt and pepper and, if desired, with grated horseradish, curry powder or mustard according to taste. Toss gently.

SERVES 6–8

Salade Catalane

225 g (8 oz) Spanish onion, peeled
olive oil
75 g (3 oz) red pepper
450 g (1 lb) cooked long-grain rice
50 g (2 oz) canned anchovy fillets, drained and diced

Dressing
6 tablespoons olive oil
2 tablespoons wine vinegar
salt
pepper

B rush the onion lightly with olive oil and bake in a moderate oven (180°C, 350°F, Gas Mark 4) for 20 minutes or until just tender, then peel and cut the onion flesh into dice. Grill the red pepper until the skin chars and blisters, then remove the skin and cut the pepper into dice.

Combine the diced onions, diced red peppers, cooked rice and drained and diced anchovy fillets. Mix together all the ingredients for the dressing, dress the salad and toss to coat all the ingredients lightly.

SERVES 8–10

Salade des Moines

350 g (12 oz) cooked long-grain rice
150 g (5 oz) cooked asparagus tips
150 g (5 oz) cooked white of chicken, cut in julienne
50 g (2 oz) truffle, grated, to garnish

Dressing
5 tablespoons olive oil
1½ tablespoons wine vinegar
1¼ teaspoons Dijon mustard

Combine the cooked rice, asparagus tips and *julienne* of white of chicken. Mix the ingredients for the dressing, season well, pour over the salad and toss. Sprinkle with grated truffle.

SERVES 6–8

Salade Monte Carlo

350 g (12 oz) cooked long-grain rice
150 g (5 oz) cooked, peeled, Dublin Bay prawns, thinly sliced
75 g (3 oz) celery heart, trimmed and thinly sliced
50 g (2 oz) truffle, sliced

Dressing
4 tablespoons olive oil
1½ tablespoons wine vinegar
2¼ tablespoons Sauce Mayonnaise, page 107
paprika

Combine all the salad ingredients. Mix together the oil and vinegar, lightly thicken with mayonnaise and season with paprika. Pour over the salad and toss.

SERVES 6–8

Salade Normande

350 g (12 oz) cooked long-grain rice
350 g (12 oz) tart dessert apples, peeled, cored and finely sliced

Dressing
4 tablespoons single cream
1½ tablespoons lemon juice
salt

pepper

ombine the cooked rice and sliced apple. Mix together the cream and lemon juice and season to taste with salt and pepper. Pour over the salad and toss.

SERVES 6–8

Salade Portugaise

350 g (12 oz) cooked long-grain rice
350 g (12 oz) tomatoes, peeled, depipped and thinly sliced
100 g (4 oz) red pepper, grilled, peeled and thinly sliced

Dressing
8 tablespoons olive oil
3 tablespoons wine vinegar
salt

pepper
a few drops anchovy essence

ombine all the salad ingredients in a bowl. Mix all the dressing ingredients, pour over the salad and toss well.

SERVES 6–8

Salade Provençale

150 g (5 oz) tomatoes, peeled and quartered
olive oil
1 clove garlic, peeled and crushed
1 tablespoon chopped fresh parsley
150 g (5 oz) aubergine, cut into large dice
85 g (3½ oz) canned anchovy fillets, drained and cut in small dice
350 g (12 oz) cooked long-grain rice

Dressing
6 tablespoons olive oil
2 tablespoons wine vinegar
salt
pepper

Season the tomatoes and fry gently in a little olive oil with the crushed garlic and parsley. Remove from the pan; add a little more oil and fry the diced aubergine until just tender. Allow both tomatoes and aubergines to cool, and place in a salad bowl with the diced anchovy fillets and rice. Mix all the ingredients for the dressing, pour over the salad and mix gently.

SERVES 6–8

Salade Réjane

225 g (8 oz) cooked long-grain rice
4 hard-boiled eggs, shelled and sliced
40 g (1½ oz) horseradish, peeled and grated
40 g (1½ oz) truffle, sliced
4 tablespoons double cream, whipped
salt

C ombine the cooked rice with the hard-boiled eggs, grated horseradish and slices of truffle. Lightly mix with the whipped cream and season with a little salt.

SERVES 4–6

Thon Marinette

225 g (8 oz) tuna fish, either fresh and poached, or canned
225 g (8 oz) small firm tomatoes, sliced
4 spring onions, trimmed and sliced
225 g (8 oz) cooked potatoes, peeled and sliced

Dressing
3 tablespoons olive oil
1 tablespoon wine vinegar
salt
pepper

S lice or flake the tuna fish neatly. Arrange overlapping slices of tuna fish, tomato and spring onion in a *ravier*, and place a border of sliced potatoes around the edge of the dish.
Mix the dressing and sprinkle over the salad.

SERVES 6

Tomates à la Génoise

8 medium tomatoes
4 small red peppers
4 small yellow peppers
6 medium potatoes, peeled, cooked and thinly sliced

Vinaigrette
6 tablespoons olive oil
2 tablespoons wine vinegar
40 g (1½ oz) anchovy fillets, chopped
pepper

Slice the tomatoes thickly and remove the pips from each slice. Grill the peppers until the skin chars and blisters, remove the skin and cut each pepper into quarters, discarding the pips.

Arrange the sliced tomatoes and quartered peppers in alternating rows in a *ravier*. Mix the olive oil and wine vinegar together with the chopped anchovies, season with pepper and sprinkle the dressing over the top. Arrange the potato slices in a border around the dish.

SERVES 6–8

Tomates à la Monégasque

16 very small tomatoes
3 tablespoons olive oil
1 tablespoon wine vinegar
salt
pepper
16 small sprigs parsley, to garnish

Stuffing
75 g (3 oz) canned tuna fish, drained and finely chopped
3 hard-boiled eggs, shelled and finely chopped
1 small onion, peeled and finely chopped
2 tablespoons chopped mixed fresh parsley, tarragon and chervil
2 tablespoons Sauce Mayonnaise, page 107

Cut off a slice from the tops of the tomatoes and remove the pips. Sprinkle the insides with a mixture of the oil, vinegar, salt and pepper, and allow to marinate for about 40 minutes.

Meanwhile, prepare the stuffing. Combine all the ingredients and stir well. Pile the stuffing into the prepared tomato cases and garnish with small sprigs of parsley.

SERVES 4–6

48

Tomates en Quartiers

16 large firm tomatoes
salt
pepper

Beurre Bercy
200 ml (7 fl oz) dry white wine
1 tablespoon finely chopped shallot
200 g (7 oz) butter, softened
500 g (1¼ lb) bone marrow, finely diced, poached and drained
3 tablespoons chopped fresh parsley
salt
pepper
juice of ½ lemon

Peel the tomatoes and cut into eight segments, cutting neatly down the tomato in a lengthwise direction. Remove the pips and allow the segments to drain well, then season lightly with salt and pepper.

To make the Beurre Bercy, place the white wine and shallot in a pan and reduce by half. Allow to cool and mix in the softened butter, the poached and drained bone marrow, 1 tablespoon parsley, salt, pepper and lemon juice.

Fill the tomato segments with Beurre Bercy using a piping bag and fancy tube. Chill in the refrigerator and garnish with the remaining chopped parsley.

Variations on this dish can be made using other butter creams. An attractive idea is to use two butter creams of contrasting colours – perhaps a pink butter cream based on prawns and a green butter cream based on the green colouring matter expressed by spinach. Fill alternate segments of tomato with cream of each colour.

SERVES 6–8

Truites Marinées

6 small trout, cleaned
Court-bouillon au Vin Blanc, page 108, modified as described
below, to cover
1 lemon, fluted and sliced

*P*oach the trout for 3–4 minutes in a very strongly flavoured Court-bouillon au Vin Blanc, made with 600 ml (1 pint) vinegar and 450 ml ($\frac{3}{4}$ pint) water instead of the 1 litre ($1\frac{3}{4}$ pints) water specified on page 108. Allow the fish to cool in the poaching liquid.

When the trout are cold, remove the skin and arrange on a serving dish with a little of the poaching liquid. Garnish with slices of fluted lemon.

Trout can also be poached in other kinds of court-bouillon made with vinegar, lemon juice or red or white wine, but the court-bouillon must always be well-acidulated. The trout can be served plainly as above but they also lend themselves to serving with any compatible sauce. The following variation provides an example.

Prepare the trout as above but this time using a modified Court-bouillon au Vinaigre, page 108, made with half water and half white wine vinegar and the rest of the flavouring ingredients as described.

Mash the yolk of 1 hard-boiled egg with a teaspoon of Dijon mustard and season with a little salt, milled pepper and a small pinch of sugar. Mix with 2 tablespoons of wine vinegar and 4 tablespoons of olive oil, then add the chopped white of the hard boiled egg and the flesh only of 2 peeled and depipped tomatoes cut into neat dice.

Place the drained and skinned trout in a serving dish and coat with this sauce; sprinkle with chopped *fines herbes* and garnish with quarters of small lettuce hearts.

SERVES 6

Filets de Truites Marinés

*75 g (3 oz) each of carrot, turnip and French beans, cut into
small dice, and peas
300 ml (½ pint) Sauce Mayonnaise, page 107
6 small trout, cleaned and poached as described opposite
lobster coral, chopped (if available)
4 hard-boiled eggs, shelled and sliced
6–8 radishes, sliced
½ cucumber, sliced*

C ook the mixed vegetables in boiling salted water, keeping
them slightly firm. Drain well. When cold, season and mix
with a scant tablespoon of the mayonnaise. Arrange this
vegetable salad as a bed in the bottom of a serving dish.

When the trout are cold, drain. Lift off the skin and carefully
remove the fillets. Coat these with mayonnaise and sprinkle
with chopped lobster coral if available.

Arrange the fillets of trout on the vegetable salad and garnish
with slices of hard-boiled egg, radish and cucumber.

SERVES 6–8

HOT
HORS D'OEUVRE

Hors d'Oeuvre Chauds

*I*n Escoffier's day, hot hors d'oeuvre sometimes figured on lunch menus together with cold hors d'oeuvre, but their real place was on the dinner menu where they came after the soup and served as a link between this and the fish and the meat main courses. In this position, as may be readily imagined, the characteristics at a premium were lightness and delicacy.

Nowadays, hot hors d'oeuvre, like their cold counterparts, are generally served at the beginning of a meal, functioning rather as an 'overture'. Although there is not the same danger of their spoiling the appetite in this position, hot hors d'oeuvre should still be light preparations to stimulate rather than satisfy the appetite.

Attereaux

An attereau consists of thin slices of various ingredients, impaled alternately on a small wooden skewer and coated with a well-reduced sauce. When the sauce has set, the attereau is trimmed, dipped in egg and breadcrumbs and deep fried at the last minute. The skewers are arranged on a serviette with a border of fried parsley, or on a bed of rice or fried bread.

Attereaux d'Huîtres à la Villeroy

36 large oysters, opened, removed from shells and bearded
36 small mushrooms
50 g (2 oz) butter
600 ml (1 pint) Sauce Villeroy, page 105
2 eggs, beaten
50 g (2 oz) fine dry breadcrumbs
oil for deep frying

To garnish
triangles of fried bread
6 sprigs fried parsley

*P*lace the oysters in a pan with their own liquor, cover and poach gently for 2–3 minutes; do not allow to boil. Meanwhile, stew the mushrooms gently in the butter until tender. Impale 6 oysters on each of 6 wooden skewers, alternating them with the cooked mushrooms.

Reduce the Sauce Villeroy with a little of the oyster poaching liquor, and coat the skewers with the well-reduced sauce. Egg-and-breadcrumb them and mould quickly into cylindrical shapes. Deep fry in hot oil (180°C, 350°F) until golden brown and serve immediately with fried bread and sprigs of fried parsley.

SERVES 6

Attereaux au Parmesan

1 litre (1¾ pints) good chicken stock
200 g (7 oz) semolina
150 g (5 oz) Parmesan, grated
120 g (4½ oz) butter
salt
pepper
grated nutmeg
175 g (6 oz) Gruyère, sliced
2 eggs, beaten
50 g (2 oz) fine dry breadcrumbs
oil for deep frying
fried parsley, to garnish

*B*ring the chicken stock to the boil, then sprinkle the semolina into it, stirring with a whisk as you do so to prevent the formation of lumps. Cook the semolina in the stock for about 30 minutes, stirring frequently, until thick. Remove from the heat and mix in the grated Parmesan cheese and 100 g (4 oz) of butter. Season with salt, pepper and nutmeg.

Butter a baking tray using the remaining butter. Spread the semolina mixture about 5 mm (¼ inch) thick on the tray, cover with buttered paper and allow to cool.

Cut into rounds using a plain 2½ cm (1 inch) pastry cutter. Also cut rounds of Gruyère cheese of the same size. Impale alternate rounds of semolina paste and Gruyère on wooden skewers. Dip the prepared skewers in beaten egg and then in breadcrumbs, and deep fry in very hot oil (190°C, 375°F) until golden brown. Arrange on a serviette with a border of fried parsley. Serve immediately.

SERVES 8

Barquettes

To avoid any confusion between barquettes and tartelettes (see page 95), both of which are made with Pâte à Foncer, Pâte pour Barquettes et Tartelettes or Feuilletage, baked to a light golden colour, it should be noted that barquettes are made in small boat-shaped moulds and tartelettes in round ones, both cut out using fancy pastry cutters. Barquettes should be used for fish and shellfish, whereas tartelettes are best used for fillings based on chicken and game.

Barquettes de Filets de Sole

225 g (8 oz) fillets of sole
40 g (1½ oz) butter
salt
pepper
squeeze of lemon juice
100 g (4 oz) mushrooms
25 g (1 oz) truffle
200 ml (7 fl oz) hot Sauce Normande, page 106
6 hot, baked barquette cases, made from Pâte à Foncer, page 96,
Pâte pour Barquettes et Tartelettes, page 97,
or Feuilletage, page 98

*P*lace the fillets of sole in a buttered baking tray and season with salt, pepper and lemon juice. Cover and cook in a moderate oven (180°C, 350°F, Gas Mark 4) for a few minutes. Meanwhile, fry the mushrooms gently in the remaining butter.

Dice the sole, mushrooms and truffle to make a *salpicon*, reserving a few slices of sole and truffle for the garnish.

Bind the salpicon with Sauce Normande and fill the barquette cases with this mixture. Coat lightly with more sauce and garnish with the reserved slices of sole and truffle.

SERVES 6

Barquettes d'Huîtres

20 oysters
150 ml (¼ pint) Sauce Béchamel, page 102
5 tablespoons fish stock
5 tablespoons double cream
a few drops lemon juice
salt and cayenne pepper
10 small, hot, baked barquette cases, made from Pâte à Foncer,
page 96, Pâte pour Barquettes et Tartelettes, page 97,
or Feuilletage, page 98
50 g (2 oz) very black truffle, chopped

R emove the oysters from their shells and poach very gently
in their own juices for 5 minutes, but do not allow to boil.
Drain and remove the beards. Reduce the Sauce Béchamel with
the fish stock, oyster cooking juices and cream to give a coating
consistency. Season with salt and cayenne pepper and add a few
drops of lemon juice.

Mix the oysters with the Sauce Béchamel and fill the
barquette cases with this, ensuring that each case contains 2
oysters. Garnish with the chopped black truffle. These
barquettes are also known as **Barquettes à l'Ostendaise**.

SERVES 4–6

Barquettes de Laitances à la Florentine

225 g (8 oz) leaf spinach
50 g (2 oz) butter
6 large soft herring roes
120 ml (4 fl oz) dry white wine
6 hot, baked barquette cases, made from Pâte à Foncer, page 96,
Pâte pour Barquettes et Tartelettes, page 97,
or Feuilletage, page 98
200 ml (7 fl oz) hot Sauce Mornay, page 103
50 g (2 oz) Parmesan, grated

Stew the spinach in the butter for 5 minutes or until tender; drain and chop roughly. Poach the herring roes in the white wine for a few minutes until tender and drain.

Cover the bottom of the barquette cases with the spinach and place a herring roe on top of each. Coat with well-seasoned Sauce Mornay and sprinkle with grated Parmesan.

Gratinate lightly under a hot grill, and serve.

SERVES 6

Beignets

The word beignet is used to describe any food, or mixture of foods, that has been dipped in frying batter and then deep fried in very hot oil to give a crisp golden brown coating. The high temperature of the oil also prevents the batter from breaking up and minimises the amount of oil absorbed by the batter.

Beignets should be arranged on a serviette and garnished with a bouquet or border of fried parsley.

Beignets à la Bénédictine

450 g (1 lb) salt cod
300 ml ($\frac{1}{2}$ pint) olive oil
1 small clove garlic, peeled and crushed
1–2 tablespoons boiling milk
salt
pepper
225 g (8 oz) dry mashed potatoes
Pâte à Frire, page 100
oil for deep frying
fried parsley, to garnish

Soak the salt cod for 12 hours under cold running water, or soak for 12 hours in water, changing the water frequently. Wash well and cut into large square pieces. Poach in fresh water for just 8 minutes from the time it comes back to the boil so as to keep the fish slightly undercooked. Drain and remove all skin and bones.

Place 100 ml (3½ fl oz) of olive oil in a shallow pan and heat until just smoking. Add the fish and crushed garlic and stir vigorously with a wooden spoon over moderate heat until the fish becomes a fairly fine paste.

Remove from the heat and add the rest of the oil, a little at a time, stirring continuously. Adjust the consistency of the paste from time to time with a little boiling milk.

The resultant paste, which is known as **Brandade de Morue**, should be very white with the consistency of mashed potato. Adjust the seasoning and add the prepared mashed potato itself.

Divide this mixture into pieces the size of a walnut and flatten each to an oval shape. Dip in frying batter and deep fry immediately in very hot oil (190°C, 375°F) until golden brown. Arrange in neat piles on a serviette with a border of fried parsley and serve.

SERVES 6–8

Beignets de Cervelle

4 pairs calf's brains
Court-bouillon au Vinaigre, page 108, to cover
6 tablespoons olive oil
juice of 1 lemon
1 tablespoon chopped fines herbes
salt
freshly ground black pepper
Pâte à Frire, page 100
oil for deep frying
fried parsley, to garnish

*P*lace the brains under gently running water to remove as much of the blood as possible, then remove all the skin and membranes and re-soak to remove the remaining blood.

Place the brains in a pan with enough vinegar court-bouillon to cover, and poach for 20–25 minutes. Allow to cool in the cooking liquid, then drain and cut into thick slices, as evenly shaped as possible. Sprinkle with the oil, lemon juice and *fines herbes*, season with salt and freshly ground black pepper and marinate for 20–30 minutes.

Dip in light frying batter and deep fry immediately in very hot oil (190°C, 375°F) until the batter is very crisp. Serve in neat piles on a serviette with a border of fried parsley.

Pig's and sheep's brains can be prepared in the same way and give equally good results, although calf's brains are considered to have a more delicate flavour. If desired, a little very finely chopped onion can be added with the oil, lemon juice and herbs for the marination of the brains.

SERVES 6

Beignets à l'Italienne

90 g (3½ oz) Parmesan, grated
1 small calf's brain, poached (see previous recipe)
225 g (8 oz) cooked white of chicken, finely diced
100 g (4 oz) lean cooked ham, finely diced
flour
Pâte à Frire, page 100
oil for deep frying

*P*ound the Parmesan to a paste with the cold cooked calf's brain and mix the diced chicken and ham into it. Divide the mixture into pieces the size of a walnut and mould into balls using a little flour. Dip in frying batter and deep fry immediately in very hot oil (190°C, 375°F) until golden brown. Arrange in neat piles on a serviette.

SERVES 8

Beignets de Laitances

225 g (8 oz) soft herring roes
Court-bouillon au Vin Blanc, page 108, to cover
3 tablespoons olive oil
juice of ½ lemon
2 tablespoons chopped parsley
Pâte à Frire, page 100
oil for deep frying

*P*oach the herring roes in the court-bouillon. Remove, then marinate for 20 minutes in the olive oil, lemon juice and parsley. Dip in batter, then deep fry immediately in very hot oil (190°C, 375°F) until golden brown. Arrange in neat piles on a serviette.

Beurrecks à la Turque

225 g (8 oz) Gruyère
3 tablespoons thick Sauce Béchamel, page 102, cooled
trimmings of Feuilletage, page 98, rolled very thinly
2 eggs, beaten
50 g (2 oz) fine white breadcrumbs
oil for deep frying

Cut the Gruyère into very small dice and mix with the thick, almost cold Sauce Béchamel. Set aside and allow this mixture to cool completely.

Shape the mixture into pieces the shape and size of a cigar and wrap each one in the very thinly rolled puff pastry trimmings to cover. Seal the edges with beaten egg, and dip in egg and then in breadcrumbs. Deep fry in hot oil (180°C, 350°F) until golden brown and serve immediately.

Beurrecks can also be made using the same ingredients and fillings as the Rissole recipes given on pages 87 and 88, but they must always be dipped in beaten egg and fine white breadcrumbs, as in the recipe above, before being deep fried.

SERVES 8

Bouchées

Bouchées (or vol-au-vent: nowadays the terms are usually interchangeable) which are being served as hors d'oeuvre are slightly smaller than usual and are sometimes called bouchées mignonnes. Their shape may be varied according to the type of filling they contain to enable guests to differentiate easily between them.

Bouchées Grand Duc

*P*repare some fancy, round vol-au-vent cases using Feuilletage, page 98. Fill with asparagus tips and truffles, cut in fairly thick short *julienne* and mixed with a little creamy Sauce Béchamel, page 102. Use slices of truffle as lids.

Bouchées Mogador

*P*repare some fancy diamond-shaped vol-au-vent cases using Feuilletage, page 98. Fill with a *salpicon* of two-thirds salt ox tongue and one-third cooked white of chicken mixed with Sauce Béchamel, page 102. Finish with a little foie gras and a little butter. Use diamond-shaped pieces of truffle as lids.

Bouchées Monseigneur

*P*repare some fancy oval-shaped vol-au-vent cases using Feuilletage, page 98. Fill with a purée of soft herring roes mixed with finely chopped truffle. Use thick diamond-shaped slices of truffle as lids.

Brochettes de Foies de Volaille

350 g (12 oz) chicken livers, cut into thick slices
salt
pepper
100 g (4 oz) butter
350 g (12 oz) mushrooms
50 g (2 oz) breadcrumbs

Dry duxelles
25 g (1 oz) butter
1 tablespoon oil
25 g (1 oz) onion, peeled and chopped
25 g (1 oz) shallot, peeled and chopped
250 g (9 oz) mushrooms, finely chopped
salt
pepper
1 pinch chopped fresh parsley

Season and sauté the chicken livers lightly in half the butter. They should stiffen and half-cook. Season and fry the mushrooms gently in the remaining butter.

To prepare the duxelles, heat the butter and oil in a pan, add the chopped onion and shallot and fry gently for a few minutes. Squeeze the mushrooms in a clean cloth to remove as much moisture as possible, then add to the pan. Cook gently until all the remaining moisture has evaporated. Season with salt and pepper and add the parsley.

Roll the chicken livers and mushrooms in the thick duxelles and impale them alternately on skewers. Sprinkle with breadcrumbs and place under a moderately hot grill to finish cooking the chicken livers.

Serve with Sauce Tomate, page 104.

SERVES 6–8

Cassolettes Alice

25 g (1 oz) butter
275 g (10 oz) cooked white of chicken, thinly sliced
300 ml (½ pint) well-reduced Sauce Velouté, page 103
1 egg, beaten

Duchesse potatoes
450 g (1 lb) potatoes, peeled
salt
50 g (2 oz) butter
pepper
grated nutmeg
2 egg yolks
1 whole egg

*F*irst prepare a duchesse potato mixture. Cut the potatoes into pieces and cook them quickly in boiling salted water, keeping them slightly firm. Drain, dry out in the oven and pass through a sieve. Replace in the saucepan and add the butter. Season to taste with salt, pepper and grated nutmeg and mix well over a low heat. Remove from the heat and stir in the egg yolks and the whole egg.

Butter 8 small shallow *cassolettes* and line with a thin layer of the duchesse potato mixture. Fill the insides with small slices of chicken mixed with the well-reduced Sauce Velouté, and cover with another layer of duchesse potato mixture cut out with a fancy cutter.

Brush with beaten egg and bake in a moderately hot oven (200°C, 400°F, Gas Mark 6) for 10–12 minutes or until the potato covering is golden brown.

SERVES 8

Ciernikis

225 g (8 oz) curd cheese
275 g (10 oz) flour, sifted
75 g (3 oz) butter, melted
3 eggs
salt
pepper
grated nutmeg

Mix together the curd cheese, 225 g (8 oz) of flour, half the melted butter, the eggs and seasonings. Pass through a fine sieve and stir in the remaining flour.

Mould into small flat cakes 4–5 cm (1½–2 inches) in diameter and 1 cm (½ inch) thick. Poach in boiling salted water for 15–18 minutes and drain well. Arrange in a hot, deep dish and sprinkle with the remaining melted butter. Serve this delicious Russian hors d'oeuvre piping hot.

Curd cheese, or tvorog, is an essential ingredient in much Russian cooking. Tvorog comes, like all Russian dairy products, in specified degrees of fatness, from fat-free to something close to cream cheese. Medium-fat, unflavoured curd cheese is ideal for this dish.

SERVES 8

Coquilles de Crevettes

225 g (8 oz) asparagus tips, steamed
25 g (1 oz) butter
50 g (2 oz) truffles, cut in a fine julienne
350 g (12 oz) prawns, cooked and shelled
450 ml ($\frac{3}{4}$ pint) hot Sauce Mornay, page 103

Duchesse potatoes
250 g (9 oz) potatoes, peeled
salt
25 g (1 oz) butter
pepper
grated nutmeg
1 egg yolk
1 whole egg

*F*irst prepare a duchesse potato mixture. Cut the potatoes into pieces and cook them quickly in boiling salted water, keeping them slightly firm. Drain, dry out in the oven and pass through a sieve. Replace in the saucepan and add the butter. Season with salt, pepper and grated nutmeg and mix well over a low heat. Remove from the heat and stir in the egg yolk and whole egg.

Pipe a border of the duchesse potato mixture round the edges of 8 scallop shells. Cover the centre of the shells with a layer of hot buttered asparagus tips mixed with a fine *julienne* of truffles and fill with hot prawns. Coat with Sauce Mornay and gratinate quickly under a hot grill.

SERVES 8

Croquets

225 g (8 oz) fresh noodles
salt
175 g (6 oz) lean cooked ham, cut in fine julienne
200 ml (7 fl oz) thick Sauce Béchamel, page 102
50 g (2 oz) Gruyère, grated
25 g (1 oz) butter
2 eggs, beaten
100 g (4 oz) fine white breadcrumbs
oil for deep frying
fried parsley, to garnish

Cook the noodles in boiling salted water, keeping them slightly firm. Drain and mix with the ham, thick Sauce Béchamel and grated cheese. Butter a baking sheet, spread the noodle mixture on this about 2 cm ($\frac{3}{4}$ inch) thick, and allow to become quite cold.

Mould the mixture into rectangles 7.5–9 cm (3–3$\frac{1}{2}$ inches) long by 4 cm (1$\frac{1}{2}$ inches) wide. Egg-and-breadcrumb the rectangles twice so as to give a double thickness of outside crust, then deep fry in very hot oil (190°C, 375°F).

Arrange on a serviette and garnish with fried parsley.

SERVES 6–8

Croquettes

The proportions of ingredients used in croquettes is crucial to their success. Although the proportions may vary, the principal ingredient, which can be poultry, game, fish or shellfish, usually determines the name of the dish and should always constitute half the total ingredients. The secondary ingredients are usually mushrooms, which account for a quarter of the ingredients; ham or tongue, one-sixth; and truffle, anything up to one-twelfth.

Thus for 500 g ($1\frac{1}{4}$ lb) *salpicon* of poultry or game, the quantity of secondary ingredients, which should also be cut in salpicon, would be 250 g (9 oz) mushrooms; 165 g ($5\frac{1}{2}$ oz) ham or tongue; and 75 g (3 oz) truffle.

These ingredients should be mixed with a thick, well-reduced sauce in keeping with the main ingredient. Here the proportions should be 400 ml (14 fl oz) of sauce to a total of 500 g ($1\frac{1}{4}$ lb) of salpicon.

When the salpicon has been mixed with the sauce, which should give a fairly stiff mixture, spread it evenly on a buttered tray and allow to become quite cold. Then divide the mixture into equal pieces, each weighing about 65 g ($2\frac{1}{2}$ oz), mould to the required shape and coat in beaten egg and breadcrumbs. Ensure that the croquettes are well coated so as to prevent them from breaking open when they are being fried, then place in very hot oil so that the egg-and-breadcrumb coating forms a strong crust.

Drain well and arrange on a serviette, garnished with fried parsley. Serve with a sauce or light *coulis* in keeping with the main ingredient.

Croquettes à l'Indienne

150 g (5 oz) long-grain rice
400 ml (14 fl oz) fish stock
400 ml (14 fl oz) Sauce Béchamel, page 102
1 teaspoon curry powder
1–2 tablespoons coconut milk
250 g (9 oz) cooked lobster meat, diced
25 g (1 oz) butter
flour
2 eggs, beaten
75 g (3 oz) fine dry breadcrumbs
oil for deep frying
fried parsley, to garnish

*P*lace the rice in a pan with the fish stock. Bring quickly to the boil, stir well and cover with a tightly fitting lid. Reduce the heat and simmer very gently for 18–20 minutes, by which time the rice should have absorbed all the liquid.

Meanwhile, flavour the Sauce Béchamel with curry powder and coconut milk, and reduce well.

When the rice is cooked, remove from the heat and gently separate the grains with a fork. Combine the rice, lobster and Sauce Béchamel. Spread the mixture on a buttered tray and allow to cool.

Divide into equal pieces each weighing about 65 g (2½ oz) and mould each into a cork shape with a little flour. Then egg-and-breadcrumb the croquettes and deep fry in very hot oil (190°C, 375°F) until golden brown. Drain well and arrange on a serviette, garnished with fried parsley. Serve with a curry sauce.

SERVES 8–10

Croquettes à la Milanaise

400 ml (14 fl oz) Sauce Béchamel, page 102
1 tablespoon tomato purée
50 g (2 oz) Parmesan, finely grated
400 g (14 oz) cooked macaroni
300 g (10½ oz) mixed julienne, comprising 150 g (5 oz) cooked
chicken breast, 100 g (3½ oz) ox tongue and 50 g (2 oz) truffle
25 g (1 oz) butter
flour
2 eggs, beaten
75 g (3 oz) fine dry breadcrumbs
oil for deep frying
fried parsley, to garnish

F lavour the Sauce Béchamel with tomato purée and grated cheese, and reduce to thicken well. Cut the cooked macaroni into small pieces, then add this and the mixed *julienne* to the Sauce Béchamel. Butter a large tray, spread the Béchamel mixture on top about 2½ cm (1 inch) thick and allow to cool.

When cold, cut into 5 cm (2 inch) squares. Coat the squares in flour, beaten egg and breadcrumbs, and deep fry in very hot oil (190°C, 375°F). Drain and arrange on a serviette with fried parsley. Serve with Sauce Tomate, page 104.

SERVES 8–10

Croquettes de Morue à l'Américaine

500 g (1¼ lb) salt cod
100 ml (3½ fl oz) thick Sauce Béchamel, page 102
flour
2 eggs, beaten
75 g (3 oz) fine dry breadcrumbs
oil for deep frying
fried parsley, to garnish

Duchesse potatoes
500 g (1¼ lb) potatoes, peeled
salt
65 g (2½ oz) butter
pepper
grated nutmeg
2 egg yolks

Soak the salt cod for 12 hours under cold running water, or soak for 12 hours in water, changing the water frequently. Cut the fish into large pieces and poach in fresh water for 10 minutes. When the fish is cooked, drain, remove all skin and bones, and flake finely.

Meanwhile, prepare a duchesse potato mixture: cut the potatoes into pieces and cook them quickly in boiling salted water, keeping them slightly firm. When the potatoes are cooked, drain, dry out in the oven and pass through a sieve. Replace in the saucepan and add the butter. Season with salt, pepper and grated nutmeg, and mix well over a gentle heat. Remove from the heat and mix in the egg yolks.

Mix the duchesse potato mixture with the flaked fish. Add the thick Sauce Béchamel and mould into balls on a well-floured surface. Brush with beaten egg, coat in breadcrumbs and deep fry. Drain and arrange on a serviette with fried parsley. Serve with a tomato sauce, such as Sauce Tomate, page 104.

SERVES 8–10

Croûtes à la Champenoise

12 slices bread, cut 2 cm ($\frac{3}{4}$ inch) thick
75 g (3 oz) clarified butter

Filling
2 pairs pig's brains
1 onion, peeled and chopped
1 clove garlic, peeled and crushed
75 g (3 oz) butter
salt
pepper

*P*lace the brains under gently running cold water to remove as much of the blood as possible, then remove all the skin and membrane and re-soak to remove the remaining blood. Drain and cut into small pieces. Gently fry the onion and garlic in the butter without colouring, then add the brains. Season with salt and pepper and cook together for 7–8 minutes. Keep the mixture hot.

Cut out 6–7 cm ($2\frac{1}{2}$–$2\frac{3}{4}$ inch) diameter rounds from the slices of bread with a plain cutter, then score an inner circle 3 mm ($\frac{1}{8}$ inch) from the edge of each round through the top surface of each slice. Fry in hot clarified butter until crisp and golden brown, then empty the insides, following the scored circle, so as to leave 12 small round cases. Reheat if necessary.

Fill with the hot mixture of brains and onion. Smooth over with a palette knife. Arrange on a serviette on a dish and serve very hot.

MAKES 12

Croûtes aux Foies de Raie

12 slices bread, cut 2 cm ($\frac{3}{4}$ inch) thick
75 g (3 oz) clarified butter

Filling
350 g (12 oz) skate livers
Court-bouillon au Vinaigre, page 108, to cover
75 g (3 oz) butter
a few drops lemon juice
1 tablespoon chopped fresh parsley

Cut out 6–7 cm ($2\frac{1}{2}$–$2\frac{3}{4}$ inch) diameter rounds from the slices of bread with a plain cutter, then score an inner circle 3 mm ($\frac{1}{8}$ inch) from the edge of each round through the top surface of each slice. Fry in hot clarified butter until crisp and golden brown, then empty the insides, following the scored circle, so as to leave 12 small round cases. Keep warm.

Bring the measured Court-bouillon au Vinaigre to the boil, add the skate livers and poach gently for a few minutes. Drain the livers well and cut into 5 mm ($\frac{1}{4}$ inch) dice. Fill the croûtes with the livers and keep warm. Cook the butter until brown, then sprinkle over the livers together with a few drops of lemon juice. Finally, sprinkle the centre of each filled croûte with a little chopped parsley.

MAKES 12

Dartois aux Anchois

350 g (12 oz) Feuilletage, page 98
100 g (4 oz) canned anchovy fillets, drained
1 egg, beaten

Whiting forcemeat
65 g (2½ oz) flour
2 egg yolks
40 g (1½ oz) melted butter
salt, pepper and grated nutmeg
120 ml (4 fl oz) boiling milk
500 g (1¼ lb) whiting, free from skin and bones
100 g (4 oz) canned anchovy fillets, drained
250 g (9 oz) softened butter

First prepare the forcemeat. Mix the flour and egg yolks together in a saucepan. Add the melted butter and seasonings and mix in the boiling milk little by little. Bring to the boil, stirring with a whisk, and allow to thicken and cook for 5–6 minutes. Remove from the heat and cool.

Pound the raw fish and add to the mixture. Pound the anchovy fillets and mix with the butter until smooth: add to the mixture and work vigorously until all the ingredients are amalgamated, then pass through a sieve.

Divide the pastry into a smaller and a larger half, then roll into strips of equal length and width, one slightly thicker than the other. Place the thinner strip on a damp baking sheet and coat with a layer of forcemeat, leaving 1 cm (½ inch) clear around the edges. Arrange thin strips of anchovy fillets in a lattice on top of the forcemeat. Moisten the edges and cover with the thicker strip of pastry. Seal the edges together and trim neatly. Brush with beaten egg and score the surface.

Bake in a hot oven (220°C, 425°F, Gas Mark 7) for 20–25 minutes. Cut into sections and arrange on a serviette.

SERVES 6–8

Dartois aux Filets de Sole

350 g (12 oz) Feuilletage, page 98
175 g (6 oz) fillets of sole, cut into thin strips
1 egg, beaten

Sole forcemeat
65 g (2½ oz) flour
2 egg yolks
40 g (1½ oz) melted butter
salt, pepper and grated nutmeg
120 ml (4 fl oz) boiling cream
500 g (1¼ lb) fillets of sole, free from skin and bones
50 g (2 oz) canned anchovy fillets, drained
250 g (9 oz) softened butter

*F*irst prepare the forcemeat. Follow the method given in the recipe opposite, but use the ingredients given above. Prepare the puff pastry as described opposite. Coat the puff pastry with the forcemeat, then cover with a lattice of strips of fillets of sole. Cover with pastry, then seal, trim, brush with beaten egg and score the surface. Bake and serve the Dartois as described opposite.

SERVES 6–8

75

Ecrevisses Farcies

100 g (4 oz) butter
50 g (2 oz) carrot, peeled and finely chopped
50 g (2 oz) onion, peeled and finely chopped
25 g (1 oz) shallot, peeled and finely chopped
5 stalks parsley
1 pinch thyme
½ bay leaf
24 raw crayfish, recently killed, washed and gutted
salt
cayenne pepper
100 ml (3½ fl oz) brandy
300 ml (½ pint) dry white wine
200 ml (7 fl oz) fish stock
200 ml (7 fl oz) thick, hot Sauce Béchamel, page 102
50 g (2 oz) fine white breadcrumbs
75 g (3 oz) butter, melted

*M*elt half the butter in a pan over a gentle heat and add the vegetables and herbs. Cover the pan and gently stew for 10 minutes or so. Add the remaining butter, the prepared crayfish, a pinch of salt and a touch of cayenne pepper. Stir over a fairly high heat until the crayfish turn red.

Warm the brandy, flame and pour over the crayfish. Add the white wine and simmer to reduce by one-third. Add the fish stock, cover the pan and simmer gently for 10 minutes.

Lift out the crayfish. Remove a wide strip of the shell along the length of the back of each crayfish using a pair of scissors. Remove the meat and cut into small dice. Reserve the shells. Remove the meat and any creamy parts from the heads and mix with the Sauce Béchamel. Pass through a fine sieve and mix with the diced meat. Pile this mixture into the reserved shells and sprinkle with fine breadcrumbs and melted butter. Gratinate quickly under a hot grill and arrange on a serviette on a dish to serve.

SERVES 6–8

Harengs à l'Esthonienne

450 g (1 lb) salted herring fillets
450 g (1 lb) white breadcrumbs
75 g (3 oz) butter
250 ml (8 fl oz) single cream
4 eggs
75 g (3 oz) clarified butter

Soak the salted herrings overnight to remove the salt. Lightly fry the breadcrumbs in butter. Purée the herring fillets and mix with the fried breadcrumbs. Add the cream and eggs, and stir the mixture well.

Cook as you would pancakes, using the clarified butter.

SERVES 6

Huîtres Favorite

16 oysters, opened
500 ml (18 fl oz) hot Sauce Béchamel, page 102
16 slices truffle
50 g (2 oz) Parmesan, grated
50 g (2 oz) butter, melted

Remove the oysters from their shells and poach very gently in their own liquor for 2–3 minutes; do not allow to boil. Wash the deeper shells thoroughly, then reserve. When the oysters are cooked, remove the beards.

Place a small spoonful of Sauce Béchamel in each of the cleaned shells, place an oyster on top and a slice of truffle on top of that. Coat with more Sauce Béchamel, sprinkle with grated Parmesan and melted butter, and gratinate each filled half shell quickly under a hot grill.

SERVES 4

Huîtres à la Florentine

16 oysters, opened
450 g (1 lb) leaf spinach
50 g (2 oz) butter
400 ml (14 fl oz) Sauce Mornay, page 103

*R*emove the oysters from their shells and poach very gently in their own liquor for 2–3 minutes; do not allow to boil. Wash the deeper shells thoroughly, then reserve. When the oysters are cooked, remove the beards.

Stew the spinach quickly in the butter for 5–10 minutes or until soft. Chop roughly. Fill each reserved oyster shell with spinach and place an oyster on top. Coat with Sauce Mornay and gratinate quickly under a hot grill.

SERVES 4

Huîtres Maréchal

16 oysters, opened
Pâte à Frire, page 100
oil for deep frying

To garnish
4 slices lemon
4 sprigs fried parsley

*R*emove the oysters from their shells and poach very gently in their own liquor for 2–3 minutes; do not allow to boil. When the oysters are cooked, remove the beards and dry well.

Dip the oysters in frying batter and deep fry in hot oil (180°C, 350°F). Arrange 4 oysters per person on a serviette on a dish and garnish with lemon and fried parsley.

SERVES 4

Pâtés à la Bourgeoise

350 g (12 oz) Feuilletage, page 98
100 g (4 oz) cooked minced beef or lamb
75 g (3 oz) mushrooms, finely chopped
1 tablespoon chopped fresh parsley
1 egg, beaten

Roll out the puff pastry about 3 mm ($\frac{1}{8}$ inch) thick and cut out 16–20 rounds with a 6 cm ($2\frac{1}{2}$ inch) pastry cutter. Use the trimmings to roll out another sheet, a little thinner than the first, and cut out the same number of rounds using the same pastry cutter.

Place the thinner rounds of pastry on a damp baking sheet and moisten the edges. Place a small spoonful of cooked minced beef or lamb, mixed with chopped raw mushrooms and parsley, in the centre of each. Cover with the other, thicker rounds of pastry and seal the edges by pressing with the back of the pastry cutter, or by crimping the edges of the pastry neatly using the back of a knife.

Brush with beaten egg and bake in a hot oven (220°C, 425°F, Gas Mark 7) for 13–15 minutes until well risen and golden brown in colour.

MAKES 16–20

Pâtés du Chanoine

16 soft herring roes
25 g (1 oz) butter
a few drops lemon juice
2 tablespoons chopped fines herbes, *blanched*
350 g (12 oz) Feuilletage, page 98
1 egg, beaten

Rinse the herring roes and place in a well-buttered, shallow pan. Lightly season, sprinkle with a few drops of lemon juice, cover with buttered paper, and poach in a moderately hot oven (190°C, 375°F, Gas Mark 5) for 7–8 minutes, or until just cooked. Allow to cool, then roll in the blanched *fines herbes*.

Roll out the puff pastry about 3 mm ($\frac{1}{8}$ inch) thick and cut out 32 small oval-shaped pieces, using an oval 9 cm ($3\frac{1}{2}$ inch) long pastry cutter. Place half the ovals on a damp baking sheet and put a poached herring roe on each. Moisten the edges, cover with the other ovals of pastry and press with the back of a slightly smaller pastry cutter to seal.

Brush with beaten egg and bake in a hot oven (220°C, 425°F, Gas Mark 7) for about 15 minutes until risen and golden brown.

MAKES 16

Piroguis en Croissants

40 g (1½ oz) butter
85 ml (3 fl oz) Jus de Veau Lié, page 101
250 g (9 oz) fine fresh rye breadcrumbs
clarified butter for frying

Tvorog
225 g (8 oz) cream cheese
225 g (8 oz) softened butter
1 egg
salt
pepper

*M*elt 25 g (1 oz) butter and add the Jus de Veau Lié and rye breadcrumbs. Stir to mix well and cook over a moderate heat until the mixture becomes very stiff. Butter a baking sheet with the remaining butter and spread the breadcrumb mixture on it 5 mm–1 cm (¼–½ inch) thick. Allow to cool.

Meanwhile, make the Tvorog. Wrap the cream cheese in a clean tea towel or piece of muslin and squeeze firmly to remove excess moisture. Place in a bowl and add the softened butter and egg. Stir with a wooden spoon until very smooth, and season to taste with salt and pepper.

Cut the cooled breadcrumb base into crescent shapes using a 6 cm (2½ inch) crescent-shaped pastry cutter dipped in hot water. Spread one side of each crescent with Tvorog and join them together in pairs. Shallow fry in clarified butter to brown lightly on both sides.

Piroguis are a classic accompaniment to many Russian soups, and are excellent with borsch. A good broth and some substantial piroguis can serve as a main supper course or lunch dish. In addition to the fillings used in this recipe and those on pages 82 and 83, chicken, chicken livers, salmon and veal can also be used to fill piroguis.

MAKES 10–12

Piroguis aux Légumes

200 g (7 oz) carrot, peeled and finely diced
40 g (1½ oz) butter
2 hard-boiled eggs, shelled and chopped
75 g (3 oz) cooked long-grain rice
250 ml (9 fl oz) thick Sauce Béchamel, page 102
450 g (1 lb) Feuilletage, page 98
1 egg, beaten

S tew the finely diced carrot in the butter until soft. Add the chopped hard-boiled eggs, cooked rice and thick Sauce Béchamel. Allow to cool.

Meanwhile, roll out the puff pastry about 3 mm (⅛ inch) thick. Cut out 32 rounds using a pastry cutter about 6 cm (2½ inches) in diameter.

Place half the pastry rounds on a damp baking sheet and put a small amount of the cold carrot mixture on each. Moisten the edges of the pastry, cover with a second round and press with the back of the pastry cutter to seal, or crimp the edges of the pastry using the back of a knife.

Brush with beaten egg and bake in a hot oven (220°C, 425°F, Gas Mark 7) for 15 minutes or until risen and golden brown.

MAKES 16

Piroguis de Smolensk

120 g (4½ oz) coarse semolina
2 eggs, beaten
900 ml (1½ pints) good chicken stock
50 g (2 oz) onion, peeled and chopped
75 g (3 oz) butter
4 hard-boiled eggs, shelled and chopped
1½ tablespoons chopped fresh parsley
450 g (1 lb) Feuilletage, page 98

*M*ix the semolina with 1 beaten egg and spread on a baking sheet. Place in a cool oven (140°C, 275°F, Gas Mark 1) to dry out for 30 minutes. Rub through a coarse sieve, then cook in the chicken stock for 20 minutes.

Meanwhile, fry the onion gently in 25 g (1 oz) butter until soft. When the semolina is cooked, drain well. Mix with the chopped hard-boiled eggs, the onion and the chopped parsley. Heat thoroughly in the remaining butter, then allow the mixture to cool completely.

Roll out the puff pastry 3 mm (⅛ inch) thick. Cut out 32 pieces measuring about 6 cm (2½ inches) square. Place half of them on a damp baking sheet and put a little of the cold prepared semolina on the centre of each one. Moisten the edges, cover with a second pastry square and seal or crimp the edges together.

Brush with beaten egg and bake in a hot oven (220°C, 425°F, Gas Mark 7) for 18 minutes until risen and golden brown.

MAKES 16

Pommes de Terre à l'Ardennaise

4 medium-size potatoes, for baking
4 egg yolks
150 g (5 oz) butter
300 g (11 oz) lean cooked ham, finely diced
100 g (4 oz) mushrooms, chopped and cooked until almost dry in
a little butter
100 g (4 oz) Parmesan, grated
salt
pepper
1 pinch grated nutmeg
1 tablespoon chopped mixed fresh parsley and chervil

Scrub the potatoes well, dry and prick all over with a fork. Bake in a moderately hot oven (200°C, 400°F, Gas Mark 6) for about 1 hour or until soft when pinched or pierced with a knife blade.

When they are cooked, cut the potatoes in half lengthways. Scoop out the insides and place in a bowl. Reserve the skins for use later.

Add the egg yolks, butter, ham, mushrooms and 75 g (3 oz) of Parmesan to the bowl. Stir with a fork and season with salt, pepper, nutmeg and herbs. Mix well together and refill the potato skins.

Smooth over the surface with a palette knife and sprinkle with the remaining grated cheese. Bake in a moderate oven (180°C, 350°F, Gas Mark 4) for 20 minutes until golden brown. Serve immediately.

These stuffed potatoes can also be served as the main course for a light supper or for an informal lunch party. If this is done, accompany the potatoes with a large mixed salad.

SERVES 8

Quiche à la Lorraine

200 g (7 oz) Pâte à Foncer, page 96
100 g (4 oz) lean bacon rashers, cut thinly
50 g (2 oz) butter
100 g (4 oz) Gruyère, thinly sliced (optional: see below)
3 eggs, beaten
300 ml ($\frac{1}{2}$ pint) single cream
salt

R oll out the pastry dough and line an 18 cm (7 inch) flan dish, taking care that the sides are a little higher than the rim of the dish.

Blanch the bacon rashers, and lightly fry in half the butter. Arrange these on the base of the flan case, alternating them with slices of Gruyère. (The use of cheese is optional and is not traditional according to local custom.)

Mix the eggs and cream and season with a pinch of salt. Pour into the flan case and dot the surface with the remaining butter, cut into small pieces.

Bake in a moderately hot oven (190°C, 375°F, Gas Mark 5) for about 30 minutes until set and golden brown. Serve while still warm.

SERVES 8

Petites Quiches au Jambon

225 g (8 oz) Pâte à Foncer, page 96
100 g (4 oz) lean cooked ham, cut thinly
400 ml (14 fl oz) single cream
3 eggs
salt
25 g (1 oz) butter, cut into small pieces

*L*ine 12 individual tartlet moulds with the pastry dough. Cut the ham into 12 small round slices and place one slice of ham in each tartlet.

Mix the cream with the eggs and a pinch of salt and fill the tartlet cases with this mixture. Dot the surface with small knobs of butter.

Bake in a moderate oven (180°C, 350°F, Gas Mark 4) for 15–18 minutes until the filling is set and the pastry is golden brown. Serve the quiches while still warm.

The ham may be cut into small dice for these 'individual portion' quiches if desired.

The use of blind-baked pastry cases for quiches does not give such a good result, in terms of texture and eating qualities, as when the whole is baked from the raw state as in this recipe.

MAKES 12

Rissoles

These are usually made up of a *salpicon*, of which the principal
ingredient can be, say, poultry, game, shellfish or foie gras,
bound in much the same way as a Croquette mixture (see page
68). Whatever the ingredients, the mixture must be quite cold
before being wrapped in a covering or envelope of pastry, such
as Pâte à Foncer, page 96, Feuilletage, page 98, or an
unsweetened brioche pastry.

Rissoles are always cooked by deep frying. They are then
arranged on a serviette and garnished with fried parsley.

Rissoles Bouquetière

100 g (4 oz) small new carrots, peeled and cut into small dice
100 g (4 oz) small new turnips, peeled and cut into small dice
50 g (2 oz) shelled peas
good chicken stock
100 g (4 oz) asparagus tips
200 ml (7 fl oz) thick Sauce Béchamel, page 102
350 g (12 oz) Feuilletage, page 98
1 egg, beaten
oil for deep frying
fried parsley, to garnish

Cook the carrots, turnips and peas in chicken stock until
tender. Drain and dry well. Steam the asparagus tips until
tender. Mix all the vegetables with the Sauce Béchamel and
allow to cool completely.

Roll and cut out the pastry dough and make rissoles, filled
with the vegetable mixture, in the shape of pleated turnovers.
Brush with beaten egg and deep fry in hot oil (180°C, 350°F)
until golden brown. Arrange on a serviette on a dish and garnish
with fried parsley.

MAKES 10

Rissoles aux Morilles

350 g (12 oz) morels, finely diced
50 g (2 oz) butter
200 ml (7 fl oz) thick Sauce Béchamel, page 102
350 g (12 oz) Pâte à Foncer, page 96
1 egg, beaten
oil for deep frying
fried parsley, to garnish

S tew the morels in the butter, then mix with the thick Sauce
Béchamel; allow to cool completely. Roll and cut out the
pastry dough and make rissoles, filled with the morel mixture,
in the shape of small round patties. Brush with beaten egg and
deep fry in hot oil (180°C, 350°F) until golden brown. Arrange
on a serviette on a dish and garnish with fried parsley.

MAKES 12–16

Rissoles à la Reine

350 g (12 oz) cooked chicken meat, finely chopped
200 ml (7 fl oz) thick Sauce Béchamel, page 102
350 g (12 oz) Feuilletage, page 98
1 egg, beaten
oil for deep frying
fried parsley, to garnish

P repare a filling of finely chopped chicken mixed with the
thick Sauce Béchamel. Roll and cut out the pastry dough
and make small turnovers filled with the chicken mixture.
  Brush with beaten egg and deep fry in hot oil (180°C, 350°F)
until golden brown. Arrange on a serviette on a dish and garnish
with fried parsley.

MAKES 12–16

Soufflés de Crustacés

225 g (8 oz) cooked prawns, crab or lobster, shelled
135 ml (4½ fl oz) Sauce Béchamel, page 102
salt
pepper
3 eggs, separated
25 g (1 oz) butter

*F*inely pound the cooked shellfish and pass through a fine sieve. Add the Sauce Béchamel, season and stir in the egg yolks. Stiffly whisk the egg whites and fold these into the shellfish mixture.

Butter 8 individual soufflé moulds and pour in the soufflé mixture. Bake in a moderately hot oven (200°C, 400°F, Gas Mark 6) for about 12 minutes, or until well risen and golden brown. Serve immediately.

These small soufflés, as well as those that follow on pages 90–93, should be cooked in small, pleated paper cases or in individual porcelain soufflé moulds (or *cassolettes*) with a capacity of approximately 100 ml (3 fl oz).

SERVES 8

Soufflés à la Florentine

100 g (4 oz) leaf spinach
50 g (2 oz) butter
salt
pepper
grated nutmeg
50 ml (2 fl oz) single cream
150 ml ($\frac{1}{4}$ pint) Sauce Béchamel, page 102
3 egg yolks
4 egg whites, stiffly beaten

Wash and finely chop the spinach. Drain well and squeeze to remove all the moisture. Cook in half the butter, with salt, pepper and nutmeg to taste, until almost dry.

Stir the cream into the hot Béchamel and reduce a little. Remove from the heat and stir in the spinach mixture and then the egg yolks, one at a time. Lightly fold in the stiffly whisked egg whites.

Butter 8 individual soufflé dishes with the remaining butter and pour in the soufflé mixture. Bake in a moderately hot oven (200°C, 400°F, Gas Mark 6) for about 12 minutes, or until well risen and golden brown. Serve immediately.

SERVES 8

Soufflés aux Huîtres

16 small oysters, opened
300 ml ($\frac{1}{2}$ pint) milk
100 g (4 oz) flour, sifted
salt
pepper
grated nutmeg
40 g (1$\frac{1}{2}$ oz) Parmesan, grated
50 g (2 oz) butter
3 eggs, separated

Remove the oysters from their shells and poach very gently in their own liquor for 2–3 minutes; do not allow to boil. When they are cooked, remove the beards.

Bring the milk to the boil and gradually stir it into the flour. Season with salt, pepper and grated nutmeg, return to the pan and bring back to the boil, stirring continuously. Add the oyster cooking liquor, then reduce slightly. Remove from the heat and add the grated Parmesan, half the butter, the egg yolks and poached oysters. Whisk the egg whites stiffly and fold in lightly.

Butter 8 individual soufflé moulds with the remaining butter and pour in the soufflé mixture, ensuring that there are 2 oysters in each one. Bake in a moderately hot oven (200°C, 400°F, Gas Mark 6) for about 12 minutes, or until well risen and golden brown. Serve immediately.

A little anchovy essence can be added to the soufflé mixture if desired, and the cheese may be omitted. The oysters may also be cut into small dice after poaching, for those people resistant to the idea of eating whole molluscs.

SERVES 8

Soufflés de Poisson

225 g (8 oz) fish fillet (see below)
salt
pepper
50 g (2 oz) butter
150 ml ($\frac{1}{4}$ pint) Sauce Béchamel, page 102
3 eggs, separated

Remove all the skin and any remaining bones from the fish fillet, then cut into dice, season and stew in half the butter until cooked. Pass through a fine sieve.

Reduce the Sauce Béchamel with a little cooking liquor from the fish, then add the sieved fish flesh. Stir in the egg yolks. Whisk the egg whites until stiff and fold in lightly.

Butter 8 individual soufflé moulds with the remaining butter and pour in the soufflé mixture. Bake in a moderately hot oven (200°C, 400°F, Gas Mark 6) for about 12 minutes, or until well risen and golden brown. Serve immediately.

This recipe is suitable for a wide number of different kinds of fish, such as salmon, sole, whiting, red mullet and smelts. The soufflé then takes its name from the fish being used, so that if salmon is used, the dish becomes **Petits Soufflés de Saumon**, and so on.

SERVES 8

Soufflés à la Suissesse

300 ml ($\frac{1}{2}$ pint) milk
100 g (4 oz) flour, sifted
salt
pepper
grated nutmeg
90 g (3$\frac{1}{2}$ oz) Parmesan, grated
75 g (3 oz) butter
3 egg yolks
2 egg whites
150 ml ($\frac{1}{4}$ pint) single cream

*B*ring the milk to the boil and gradually stir it into the flour. Season with salt, pepper and grated nutmeg, return to the pan and bring back to the boil, stirring continuously.

Remove from the heat and add 40 g (1$\frac{1}{2}$ oz) of grated Parmesan, 25 g (1 oz) of butter and the egg yolks. Whisk the egg whites until stiff and fold in lightly.

Use another 25 g (1 oz) butter to grease 8 individual soufflé moulds and pour in the prepared soufflé mixture. Place in a shallow ovenproof dish with a little hot water in the bottom and bake in a moderately hot oven (200°C, 400°F, Gas Mark 6) for 15 minutes, taking care that the water does not boil.

Meanwhile, butter a deep ovenproof serving dish with the remaining butter and sprinkle with 25 g (1 oz) Parmesan. Turn the soufflés out on to the dish and sprinkle with the remaining Parmesan. Pour the cream into the dish to come halfway up the soufflés and return to the oven to bake for a further 12 minutes, or until all the cream has been absorbed and the soufflés are golden brown. Serve immediately.

SERVES 8

Subrics Piémontais

50 g (2 oz) onion, peeled and chopped
50 g (2 oz) butter
120 g (4½ oz) arborio rice
250 ml (8 fl oz) chicken stock
50 g (2 oz) Parmesan, grated
2 eggs, beaten
50–75 g (2–3 oz) clarified butter

*F*ry the onion gently in half the butter until soft and golden brown. Add the rice and stir over a moderate heat until it becomes well impregnated in butter.

Moisten with the chicken stock, cover and cook the rice in a moderate oven (180°C, 350°F, Gas Mark 4) for 18 minutes. When the rice is cooked, stir in the remaining butter, the grated Parmesan and the beaten eggs. Check the seasoning, adjusting if necessary.

Heat enough clarified butter to cover the bottom of a small pan and drop 50 g (2 oz) spoonfuls of the rice mixture into the hot fat. Cook the subrics for about 2 minutes on each side until golden brown. Arrange on a serviette on a dish and serve very hot.

MAKES 10–14

Tartelettes Châtillon

225 g (8 oz) mushrooms, sliced
25 g (1 oz) butter
200 ml (7 fl oz) hot Sauce Béchamel, page 102
10 hot, baked tartlet cases, made from Pâte à Foncer, page 96,
Pâte pour Barquettes et Tartelettes, page 97, or Feuilletage,
page 98

Chicken forcemeat
175 g (6 oz) chicken breast meat, trimmed
salt and white pepper
$\frac{1}{2}$ egg white
150 ml ($\frac{1}{4}$ pint) double cream

First prepare the chicken and cream forcemeat. Pound the chicken until fine with the seasonings, then pound in the egg white, or work all together in a food processor. Pass through a fine sieve. Chill thoroughly, then add the cream, a little at a time, working well until smooth and light.

Sauté the sliced mushrooms in the butter and mix with the Sauce Béchamel. Partly fill the tartlet cases with this mixture, then cover with a thin layer of the forcemeat. Place on a baking sheet and bake in a moderate oven (180°C, 350°F, Gas Mark 4) for 15–20 minutes, or until the forcemeat is cooked. Serve arranged on a serviette on a dish.

Tartelettes a la Reine are very similar to these tartlets. Line baked tartlet cases with a thin layer of chicken forcemeat, then cook for a few moments in a moderate oven (180°C, 350°F, Gas Mark 4). Fill with thin slices of uncooked white of chicken, mushroom and truffle mixed with a little **Sauce Suprême** (Sauce Velouté, page 103, reduced and finished with double cream). Cover with more forcemeat and return to the oven to finish cooking.

MAKES 10

BASIC RECIPES

Pâte à Foncer

250 g (9 oz) flour, sifted
1 pinch salt
125 g (4½ oz) butter, softened
50 ml (2 fl oz) water

*M*ake a well in the flour and place the salt, butter and water in the centre. Mix the flour gradually into the butter and water until it is incorporated and forms a paste. Mix the pastry dough together for a moment, then press it firmly between the palm of the hand and the worktop, pushing small pieces away from the main ball of dough with the heel of the hand, thus assuring the complete blending of all the ingredients. Do this twice. Form into a ball then wrap in a cloth and place in the refrigerator, preferably for a few hours, before use.

MAKES APPROXIMATELY 400 G (14 OZ)

Pâte pour Barquettes et Tartelettes

250 g (9 oz) flour, sifted
salt
125 g (4½ oz) butter, melted and cooled
1 egg
2 egg yolks
a few drops water

Combine the sifted flour and a pinch of salt with the melted butter, egg, egg yolks and a few drops of water. Quickly mix to a paste, handling it as little as possible. Roll into a ball, then press it firmly between the palm of the hand and the worktop, pushing small pieces away from the main ball of dough with the heel of the hand, thus assuring the complete blending of all the ingredients. Do this twice. Form into a ball again, then wrap in a cloth and place in the refrigerator, preferably for a few hours, before use.

To use this pastry dough, the pastry dough opposite, and the Feuilletage on page 98 to make pastry cases, line the moulds with the required dough rolled out fairly thinly. Prick the pastry dough well with a fork, then allow it to rest for at least 30 minutes in a cool place or in the refrigerator. Line the case with foil or greaseproof paper, then fill it with dried or ceramic beans, and bake blind in a moderately hot oven (200°C, 400°F, Gas Mark 6) for 10–15 minutes, or until light golden brown. The case should then be emptied of beans and returned to the oven for a few minutes more so that the base can dry out fully. This will prevent the pastry from absorbing too much moisture from the filling.

MAKES APPROXIMATELY 400 G (14 OZ)

Feuilletage

250 g (9 oz) strong flour
1 pinch salt
150 ml ($\frac{1}{4}$ pint) cold water
250 g (9 oz) butter

S ift the flour and salt together into a mixing bowl or onto a marble surface and make a well in the centre. Add the cold water and mix to a paste. Roll into a ball without working it too much and leave to rest for 20 minutes.

Meanwhile, work the butter until it has the same texture as the dough. Roll the paste out evenly to form a 15 cm (6 inch) square of even thickness. Place the well-kneaded butter in the centre and fold over the edges of the paste to enclose it completely, thus forming a square block. Allow this package to rest for at least 20 minutes.

Roll out the paste and give it two turns, as follows. First of all, roll it out to form an oblong 40 cm (16 inches) long by 15 cm (6 inches) wide, then fold it in three. Turn this package through 90° and roll out and fold as before. Turn the package through 90° again.

Allow the paste to rest for a further 10 minutes in the refrigerator, then roll the dough out twice more, turning the package through 90° after each folding. Allow to rest for another 10 minutes or so in the refrigerator and then repeat the procedure again.

After six turns, and 30 minutes' rest in the refrigerator, the puff pastry is ready for use. Any trimmings left over after use should be reassembled into a ball and kept in the refrigerator. They can be used to make small bouchées, barquettes, and other delicate hors d'oeuvre pastries.

MAKES APPROXIMATELY 650 G (1 LB 7 OZ)

Pâte à Choux

250 ml (8 fl oz) water
100 g (4 oz) butter
salt
150 g (5 oz) strong flour, sifted
4 medium eggs
1 egg, beaten

*P*lace the water in a pan with the butter and a pinch of salt. Bring to the boil slowly so that the butter is melted by the time the water boils. Remove from the heat, add the flour and mix well together with a wooden spatula. Return to the heat and beat well until the pastry leaves the sides of the pan cleanly.

Remove from the heat again and allow to cool slightly. Add the eggs, one at a time, beating each in well to incorporate. After all four eggs have been added, the mixture should just hold its own shape when piped.

To use this pastry dough, pipe appropriately sized balls of dough on to a lightly buttered baking sheet, using a piping bag fitted with a plain tube. Brush with the beaten egg and bake in a moderately hot oven (200°C, 400°F, Gas Mark 6) for approximately 20–25 minutes until crisp and light brown in colour. Place on a wire rack to cool.

MAKES APPROXIMATELY 700 G ($1\frac{1}{2}$ LB)

Pâte à Frire

125 g (4½ oz) flour, sifted
1 pinch salt
25 ml (1 fl oz) olive oil or melted butter
200 ml (7 fl oz) lukewarm water
2 egg whites

*I*f the batter is required for immediate use, place all the ingredients except for the egg whites in a basin and mix by turning them over gently with a wooden spoon, without working the batter in any way. This will prevent the batter from becoming elastic (an elastic batter will not stick to the items of food dipped into it).

If the batter is prepared in advance, on the other hand, all the ingredients except for the egg whites can be mixed well and then allowed to rest for a while – preferably at least 1 hour – during which time the batter will lose its elasticity.

Whisk the egg whites stiffly and fold these into the batter immediately before use.

MAKES APPROXIMATELY 450 ML (¾ PINT)

Jus de Veau Lié

4 litres (7 pints) good veal or beef stock
25 g (1 oz) arrowroot

R eserve 100 ml ($3\frac{1}{2}$ fl oz) of the cold stock for use later. Bring the rest of the stock to the boil, then allow it to reduce to a quarter of its original volume.

Dilute the arrowroot in the reserved cold stock, stir into the boiling stock and allow to cook gently for 1 minute. Pass through a fine strainer. The resultant gravy should be transparent and light brown in colour, and have a fresh, clean aroma and taste.

MAKES APPROXIMATELY 1 LITRE ($1\frac{3}{4}$ PINTS)

Cuisson de Champignons

450 g (1 lb) white mushrooms, finely chopped
juice of $\frac{1}{4}$ lemon
25 g (1 oz) butter
1 pinch salt
50 ml (2 fl oz) water

P lace the mushrooms in a pan with the lemon juice, butter, salt and water. Cover, heat slowly and simmer for a few minutes only. Squeeze firmly through muslin or a very fine strainer to extract all the liquid.

MAKES APPROXIMATELY 150 ML ($\frac{1}{4}$ PINT)

Sauce Béchamel

65 g (2½ oz) butter
65 g (2½ oz) flour, sifted
1 litre (1¾ pints) boiling milk
1 onion, peeled and finely sliced
1 sprig thyme
salt
pepper
1 pinch grated nutmeg

*F*irst prepare a white roux by mixing together 50 g (2 oz) of the butter and the flour in a heavy pan and placing over moderate heat for just a few minutes, stirring frequently, to eliminate the raw flavour of the flour. Allow to cool.

Gradually stir the milk into the roux so as to obtain a smooth sauce and bring to boiling point. Fry the onion gently in the remaining butter but do not allow to brown, then add the thyme, salt, pepper and grated nutmeg. Add this mixture to the sauce and simmer for 1 hour. Pass through a fine strainer.

If you are not going to use the sauce immediately, coat the surface with a little butter to prevent a skin forming. For the thick or very thick Sauce Béchamel required for certain recipes, allow to simmer and reduce considerably before straining and using. For a light Sauce Béchamel, thin with a little boiling milk before straining and using.

Whenever Sauce Béchamel is used as the basis for a sauce to accompany a poached item of food, or an item of food whose cooking has produced a liquid, this liquid should be added to the Béchamel and reduced to the required consistency.

It should be remembered that this sauce is one of the most useful and versatile in the European cookery tradition. The utmost care should therefore be given to its preparation. The making of Sauce Béchamel should never be regarded as an irksome chore.

MAKES APPROXIMATELY 900 ML (1½ PINTS)

Sauce Velouté

50 g (2 oz) butter
65 g (2¼ oz) flour, sifted
1 litre (1¾ pints) white stock or fish stock depending on the flavour
of the dish in preparation

*F*irst prepare a white roux by mixing the butter and flour together in a heavy pan and placing over a moderate heat for just a few minutes, stirring frequently, to eliminate the raw flavour of the flour. Allow to cool.

Gradually stir the stock into the roux, making sure that you obtain a smooth consistency. Bring to the boil, stirring continuously, and allow to simmer very gently for 1 hour, skimming carefully from time to time. Strain and use as required.

MAKES APPROXIMATELY 900 ML (1½ PINTS)

Sauce Mornay

100 ml (3½ fl oz) milk, stock or cooking liquor
1 litre (1¾ pints) Sauce Béchamel, page 102
25 g (1 oz) Gruyère, grated
25 g (1 oz) Parmesan, grated
50 g (2 oz) butter

*A*dd the milk, stock or the cooking liquor from the dish with which the sauce is to be served to the Sauce Béchamel. Reduce by a third and add all the grated cheese.

Reheat for a few seconds, mix well to ensure that the cheese is melted, and finish with the butter.

MAKES APPROXIMATELY 900 ML (1½ PINTS)

Sauce Tomate

15 g ($\frac{1}{2}$ oz) butter
25 g (1 oz) streaky bacon, diced and blanched
25 g (1 oz) onion, peeled and roughly diced
40 g (1$\frac{1}{2}$ oz) carrot, peeled and roughly diced
1 bay leaf
1 sprig thyme
25 g (1 oz) flour
1.5 kg (3 lb 6 oz) ripe tomatoes, squashed
400 ml (14 fl oz) white stock
1 clove garlic, peeled and crushed
1 pinch caster sugar

Melt the butter in a flameproof casserole, then add the bacon and fry gently. Add the vegetables and herbs and fry until golden brown. Sprinkle with the flour and stir. Cook until golden brown and allow to cool. Add the rest of the ingredients, season, then bring to the boil, stirring continuously. Cover with a lid and place in a moderate oven (170°C, 325°F, Gas Mark 3) for 1$\frac{1}{2}$–2 hours, then strain into a clean pan. Return to the boil for a few minutes. If not for immediate use, coat the surface with butter to prevent a skin forming.

MAKES APPROXIMATELY 1 LITRE (1$\frac{3}{4}$ PINTS)

Sauce Allemande

275 ml (9 fl oz) white stock
100 ml (3½ fl oz) Cuisson de Champignons, page 101
3 small egg yolks
a squeeze lemon juice
1 pinch each coarsely ground black pepper and grated nutmeg
500 ml (18 fl oz) Sauce Velouté, page 103
50 g (2 oz) butter

*P*lace all the ingredients except the Sauce Velouté and the butter in a heavy, shallow pan. Mix well, then add the Sauce Velouté. Bring to the boil, stirring continuously, then reduce the heat and cook until the sauce has reduced by one-third and will just coat the back of the spoon. Pass through a fine strainer. Cut the butter into small pieces and whisk it into the sauce before serving.

If you are not going to use the sauce immediately, coat the surface with 15 g (½ oz) butter, keep warm in a bain-marie and whisk in the remaining butter just before serving.

MAKES APPROXIMATELY 600 ML (1 PINT)

Sauce Villeroy

150 ml (¼ pint) ham-flavoured white stock
500 ml (18 fl oz) Sauce Allemande (above)
2 tablespoons truffle essence

*R*educe the white stock until only 2 tablespoons are left, then add the Sauce Allemande and the truffle essence. Reduce rapidly, stirring continuously, until a thick, coating consistency is reached. Allow to cool slightly before use.

MAKES APPROXIMATELY 300 ML (½ PINT)

Sauce Normande

3 egg yolks
150 ml ($\frac{1}{4}$ pint) double cream
350 ml (12 fl oz) Sauce Velouté, page 103, made with fish stock
50 ml (2 fl oz) Cuisson de Champignons, page 101
50 ml (2 fl oz) mussel cooking liquor
100 ml (4 fl oz) fish stock
a squeeze lemon juice
65 g (2$\frac{1}{2}$ oz) butter

Combine the egg yolks with 50 ml (2 fl oz) of the cream and place in a pan with the Sauce Velouté, the mushroom and mussel cooking liquors, the fish stock and the lemon juice. Stir well together and bring to the boil.

Allow the sauce to reduce by one-third, stirring continuously, then pass through a fine strainer. Finish the sauce with the remaining cream and the butter. Check the seasoning, adjusting if necessary.

In addition to its specified uses in this book, this creamy fish sauce also makes an excellent accompaniment for poached white fish, especially sole. The fish stock should be based on trimmings of the fish in preparation.

MAKES APPROXIMATELY 500 ML (18 FL OZ)

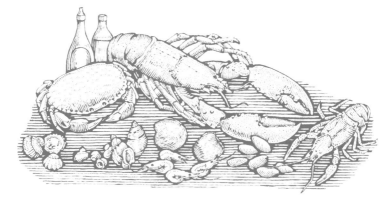

Sauce Mayonnaise

2 egg yolks
salt
white pepper
$\frac{1}{2}$ tablespoon wine vinegar or lemon juice
300 ml ($\frac{1}{2}$ pint) olive oil
2 tablespoons boiling water

*W*hisk the egg yolks in a basin with the seasonings and a little of the vinegar or lemon juice. Add and whisk in the oil, drop by drop to begin with, then faster in a stream, as the sauce begins to thicken. Adjust the consistency occasionally by adding a few more drops of vinegar or lemon juice.

Lastly, add the water, which ensures that the emulsification holds, even if the sauce is not used immediately.

MAKES APPROXIMATELY 400 ML (14 FL OZ)

Sauce Moutarde à la Crème

25 g (1 oz) dry mustard
salt
pepper
a few drops lemon juice
300 ml ($\frac{1}{2}$ pint) double cream

*P*lace the mustard, a pinch of salt and pepper and a few drops of lemon juice in a bowl. Mix well. Gradually add the double cream, drop by drop, as when making mayonnaise.

MAKES 300 ML ($\frac{1}{2}$ PINT)

Court-bouillon au Vinaigre

1 litre (1¾ pints) water
50 ml (2 fl oz) white wine vinegar
10 g (⅓ oz) coarse salt
125 g (4½ oz) carrot, peeled and sliced
100 g (4 oz) onion, peeled and sliced
1 sprig thyme
½ bay leaf
20 g (¾ oz) chopped fresh parsley
a few peppercorns

P lace all the ingredients in a pan except for the peppercorns. Bring to the boil and simmer gently for about 1 hour. Add the peppercorns 10 minutes before the end, then strain. The court-bouillon is now ready for use.

MAKES APPROXIMATELY 1 LITRE (1¾ PINTS)

Court-bouillon au Vin Blanc

1 litre (1¾ pints) water
1 litre (1¾ pints) white wine
225 g (8 oz) onion, peeled and sliced
40 g (1½ oz) parsley stalks
1 sprig thyme
1 small bay leaf
25 g (1 oz) coarse salt
10 g (¼ oz) peppercorns

P lace all the ingredients except for the peppercorns in a pan, bring to the boil and simmer gently for 20 minutes. Then add the peppercorns, simmer for a further 10 minutes and strain. The court-bouillon is now ready for use.

MAKES APPROXIMATELY 1.75 LITRES (3 PINTS)

GLOSSARY

bâtons food such as carrot or turnip cut into small neat sticks, approximately 2 cm ($\frac{3}{4}$ inch) in length and 3 mm ($\frac{1}{8}$ inch) square.

beurre manié a mixture of one part flour to one-and-a-half or two parts soft butter mixed to a smooth paste, and used to thicken sauces towards the end of the cooking period.

cassolettes small ovenproof dishes in different shapes used for the cooking and serving of small entrées and hors d'oeuvre.

coulis a thick sauce or purée made from vegetables or fruits.

dariole a small, narrow mould with sloping sides, used to set creams and jellies, and to bake certain desserts.

fines herbes a mixture of chopped fresh parsley, chervil, tarragon and chives.

julienne items of food cut into regular, matchstick-sized strips.

paupiettes slices of meat or fillets of fish, spread with a forcemeat and rolled up before cooking.

ravier a small dish specifically used for the serving of hors d'oeuvre.

salpicon cooked food cut into small regular dice, and usually mixed with a sauce or forcemeat as binding agent.

INDEX